JEAN-JACQUES ROUSSEAU

JEAN-JACQUES ROUSSEAU

RONALD GRIMSLEY

*Emeritus Professor of French,
University of Bristol*

THE HARVESTER PRESS · SUSSEX

BARNES & NOBLE BOOKS · NEW JERSEY

First published in Great Britain in 1983 by
THE HARVESTER PRESS LIMITED
Publisher: John Spiers
16 Ship Street, Brighton, Sussex

and in the USA by
BARNES & NOBLE BOOKS
81 Adams Drive, Totowa, New Jersey 07512

British Library Cataloguing in Publication Data

Grimsley, Ronald
    Jean-Jacques Rousseau.
    1. Rousseau, Jean-Jacques
    I. Title
    194   B2137

    ISBN 0-7108-0051-7

Library of Congress Cataloging in Publication Data

Grimsley, Ronald.
    Jean-Jacques Rousseau.

    1. Rousseau, Jean-Jacques, 1712-1778.   I. Title.
B2137.G69   1983   194   82-24409
ISBN 0-389-20378-5

Typeset in 11 on 12 point Times by
Alacrity Phototypesetters, Banwell Castle, Weston-super-Mare.
Printed in Great Britain by
The Thetford Press Limited, Thetford, Norfolk

THE HARVESTER PRESS PUBLISHING GROUP
The Harvester Press Publishing Group comprises Harvester Press Limited
(chiefly publishing literature, fiction, philosophy, psychology, and science
and trade books), Harvester Press Microform Publications Limited (publishing in microform unpublished archives, scarce printed sources, and
indexes to these collections) and Wheatsheaf Books Limited (a wholly independent company chiefly publishing in economics, international politics,
sociology and related social sciences), whose books are distributed by The
Harvester Press Limited and its agencies throughout the world.

To Valerie

Contents

1. Rousseau and the French Enlightenment

The sight of his name in histories of philosophy would undoubtedly have aroused contradictory feelings in Rousseau: grateful to learn that his ideas were at last being given the serious consideration he believed they deserved, he would also have remembered his frequent denunciation of contemporary thinkers and his firm refusal to describe himself as a 'philosopher'. To the Archbishop of Paris, who had launched a pastoral letter against *Emile*, he wrote: 'I have never aspired to this title [of philosopher] to which I recognize that I have no right, and I assuredly do not give it up through modesty' (IV, 1004).[1] 'I have never aspired to become a philosopher', he wrote on another occasion, 'I have never claimed to be one; I was not, am not and do not want to become one' (*CC*, IX, 140).[2] If he was not 'a great philosopher and had no desire to be one', it was because he saw himself as a 'simple, truthful man' who 'sometimes had common sense and loved the truth'. He treated his rejection of 'philosophy' as a convincing proof of his own sincere attachment to the pursuit of wisdom.

As well as castigating the 'philosophers' of his time, Rousseau was also opposed to traditional metaphysics and in this respect he did not greatly differ from other thinkers of the French Enlightenment who rejected the abstract, rationalistic outlook inspired by Descartes in favour of an appeal to experience and observation. Although Descartes was still considered as a great pioneer who had courageously freed philosophy from the irksome constraint of scholastic authority and, through his method of doubt, had urged men to think for themselves, he was blamed for having betrayed his own rational principles: his pursuit of philosophical certainty and absolute truth had led him to construct a metaphysical system that ultimately owed little to the critical outlook expounded in the *Discourse on Method*. This characteristic eighteenth-

1

century view of a great innovator who had finally pursued an intellectual will o' the wisp is effectively illustrated in Voltaire's *Philosophical Letters* of 1734: there Descartes is praised for having 'given sight to the blind' and exposed the 'faults of antiquity'; 'born to discover the errors of antiquity, he destroyed the absurd fancies with which youth had been infatuated for two thousand years and he taught the men of his time to reason and to use his [Descartes's] arms against himself'. Unfortunately, however, he replaced ancient errors by his own and 'allowed himself to be carried away by this systematic spirit which blinds the greatest men', so that he ultimately followed his imagination rather than his reason, thereby producing a mere 'romance' instead of a valid philosophical work. Destined to become an egregious example of philosophical system-building, his philosophy was nothing but 'an ingenious romance and credible only to the ignorant'.

As Voltaire emphasises in the same work, Descartes's constructive philosophy had been convincingly discredited by the achievements of two great thinkers whom the Enlightenment was to treat as 'demi-gods': John Locke and Isaac Newton. Modern philosophy had at last been set on the right path — such was the view accepted by nearly all the major thinkers of the French Enlightenment — by John Locke, who was treated as its true founder. In Voltaire's words, after 'so many reasoners had produced the romance of the soul', Locke, with his 'wise, methodical and exact' approach, had seen that the philosopher's true task was to trace 'the history of the human mind' by showing how 'all our ideas come to us through the senses' and are stimulated through contact with the physical world. He thus destroyed the Cartesian concept of innate ideas and the pretensions of traditional metaphysics. Henceforth men would have to be content with the careful analysis of ideas which came within the range of their immediate experience; instead of building metaphysical systems, they had to accept the limitations of human knowledge and concentrate on examining the genesis of ideas. It was only when the mind recognized its inability to reach absolute truth and penetrate the ultimate nature of reality that genuine philosophical progress would be possible.

An equally decisive blow to Descartes's influence had been

delivered by the remarkable scientific achievements of New-ton, to whom Voltaire also devotes considerable space in the *Philosophical Letters*.[3] Descartes had always maintained that science was inseparable from its metaphysical foundations and that, without firm philosophical presuppositions, it could make little progress. Newton, on the other hand, had brilliant-ly shown the remarkable results of a scientific attitude that eschewed metaphysical hypotheses in favour of a mathemati-cal approach carefully controlled by observation and experi-ment. However eloquently Descartes may have argued in favour of such notions as the vortices and the *plenum*, Newton had not only proved that they were incompatible with scienti-fic facts, but had brought about a scientific revolution with a theory of gravitation that did not rest on abstract arguments but on the analysis of observable effects.

Although, as we shall have occasion to see, the *philosophes* to some extent still remained under the influence of the rationalist spirit they so frequently criticised, they undoubtedly desired to bring philosophy closer to experience. The article 'Philosopher' in the *Encyclopaedia* of Diderot and d'Alembert provides a good example of this change of attitude. The author (perhaps the grammarian Dumarsais) insists that 'reason is to the philosopher what grace is to the Christian'. Unlike other men who 'walk in darkness', the true philosopher forms his principles on 'an infinity of particular observations'; he 'takes the maxim at its source and examines its origin, stresses its true value and makes appropriate use of it'. The 'philosophical spirit' is based on an attitude of 'observation and precision which relates everything to its true principles'. Equally sig-nificant is the philosopher's involvement with life, for he does not consider himself to be 'an exile in this world' or 'in enemy territory'. On the contrary, he is *un honnête homme* who wants to please others and make himself useful to them. This means that 'our philosopher, who knows how to divide himself between seclusion and human intercourse, is full of humanity'. He lives close to civil society which is for him 'a divinity on earth', so that he pays scrupulous attention to his duties. Since feelings of probity are as important as intellectual understand-ing or an enlightened mind, his moral and rational attitudes will make him support toleration and reject fanaticism. At the same time he will respect freedom, order and rule as he works for the good of society.

Other eighteenth-century attempts to define the 'philosopher' reveal this widening of outlook which is now stressed by modern English-speaking critics who use the term '*philosophe*' to describe the typical thinker of the French Enlightenment. Whether for good or ill, the *philosophe* was deeply involved with the affairs of society and he could no longer consider himself a lonely thinker pondering deeply abstract problems in the remoteness of his study. Because knowledge was deemed to be important for its effect upon human life, the genuine thinker was henceforth impelled to abandon the sterility of metaphysical speculation for the advantages of what was widely described as the 'philosophical spirit' — an outlook that was relevant not only to the analysis of intellectual problems but also to man's existence in the world.

The first and most obvious characteristic of this new philosophical spirit was its strongly critical aspect and this is why many critics have seen in the *philosophes* the heirs of the 'free-thinkers' (or *libertins*) of the previous century and the *libres-penseurs* of the modern period. It would obviously be misleading to limit the emergence of this new spirit to any single source, for it was so widely 'iffused that it became part of the general 'progressive' outlook of the time. In any case, a new critical outlook had been developing in Europe since the time of the Renaissance (the eighteenth century had considerable affection and respect for Montaigne) and it had already found eloquent spokesmen in such thinkers as Bayle and Fontenelle, whose thought had been formed before the work of Locke and Newton became widely known. Bayle, with his *Historical and Critical Dictionary* of 1697, had shown the devastating effects of historical criticism upon many traditional religious beliefs, while as early as 1687 Fontenelle's *History of Oracles* had adopted a sceptical attitude towards Christian miracles, and his *Conversations on the Plurality of Worlds* (1686) had begun to make scientific subjects available to a wide public.

The attack upon the old absolutes was not restricted to metaphysics but rapidly involved a more sustained and vigorous onslaught on what was judged to be a still greater obstacle

4

to the growth of enlightenment — Christianity, especially in its Roman Catholic form. In France the frequently close relationship between King and Church and the continued power — sometimes faltering, always menacing and frequently oppressive — of the Old Regime meant that writers had to contend with a politically and ecclesiastically-inspired censorship which condemned freedom of speech as a grave challenge to traditional moral, religious and social values. Since loyalty to Christian principles meant strict obedience to the authority of the Church, it is not surprising to find the Jesuits in their *Dictionary of Trévoux* referring to the new thinkers as men who 'put themselves above the obligation of a Christian existence and the life of the citizen and who, by pretending to be free from all prejudices, mock those who respect established laws'.

In the eyes of the *philosophes*, accepting the *esprit philosophique* meant putting 'nature' above the supernatural. Their fierce opposition to the constraints imposed by religious orthodoxy was inspired by the conviction that they were fighting for man's happiness in this world and not in the next. 'Nature' might be difficult to define, but in most thinkers' minds it was inseparable from a rejection of revealed religion. If the examples of Locke and Newton were so inspiring (and most French thinkers ignored their professed loyalty to the Christian tradition), it was partly because of their achievement as thinkers who had been able to make free and untrammelled use of their mental resources. One of Voltaire's main points in the *Philosophical Letters* had been to stress the cultural benefits of English liberalism. Whereas Descartes had been forced to leave France because of his fear of possible persecution, Newton had become a source of national pride and had been buried in Westminster Abbey. For Voltaire it was significant that so many English writers and thinkers should be appointed to influential official posts which, to a large extent, were considered as rewards for their services to science and letters. In the same way the religious freedom enjoyed by the English was in remarkable contrast to the striking intolerance that existed in France. Voltaire pointed out that philosophers, unlike their religious and political counterparts, did not want to become leaders of sects or factions. Philosophers, he averred, would never form a religious sect because they did not seek to foment popular passions or to encourage fanaticism; their love of truth and wisdom meant they were without that 'enthusiasm' which Locke had attributed to 'the conceits of a warmed or overweening brain', more dangerous in its effects on the 'persuasions and actions of men' than those of 'reason and divine revelation'.[4]

To trust in nature was to make use of one of its most remarkable attributes — reason. Moreover, as Locke and Newton had so convincingly demonstrated, reason, when properly used, could bring positive benefits to mankind, for, as well as destroying prejudices, it could be used to spread enlightenment and speed up cultural progress. In view of this, it is not surprising that this new rational spirit should find its most constructive expression in the domain of science. Few of the *philosophes* were practising scientists (Buffon was a conspicuous exception and he never considered himself as a true *philosophe*) but all admired the intellectual and practical achievements of contemporary science. Newton's brilliant success seemed to offer an almost unlimited hope of extending man's knowledge and control of his physical world. Although there was as yet little sign of the emergence of the 'positivist' spirit that was to appear a century later, the scientist was henceforth to occupy a privileged position among the benefactors of humanity; in the *philosophes*' opinion it was only by imitating his fidelity to observation and experiment that modern thinkers could hope to further the cause of enlightenment. Since Locke's empiricism stressed the importance of a genetic approach to philosophical problems, it was widely held that philosophy and science could combine very effectively to explain hitherto unsolved problems concerning man's existence.

The strongly critical and rational aspects of the new 'philosophical spirit' were clearly not concerned with intellectual issues alone; because he wanted to enlighten men who were struggling to solve the problem of living in this world rather than in the next, the new *philosophe* was deeply involved with practical as well as theoretical problems. The emphasis on the supremacy of 'nature' meant that the aim of human life was henceforth to find happiness as well as truth. It followed that nature was not simply a philosophical principle and the source of all rational and scientific investigation but also a criterion which could be used for the elimination of oppression and injustice. The critical mood of the Enlightenment did not condemn outworn ideas simply because they were irrational, but also because they were inhuman. If the Church thought that its oppressive methods were a means of safeguarding the truth, the *philosophes* considered them to be an affront to human dignity and an encouragement to fanaticism; in their opinion religious truth ought to rest on its own intrinsic value and not on the power of a ruthlessly intolerant ecclesiastical and social organisation. In the same way the *philosophe*, though certainly not a revolutionary, was anxious to remove social and political abuses which were contrary to the well-being of enlightened humanity. Such was the case, for example, with the barbarous features of the penal code. Voltaire, as is well known, was not content merely to write a commentary on the Italian publicist Beccaria's reforming treatise *On Crimes and Punishments*, but campaigned vigorously to clear the names of victims of legal injustice such as Calas, Sirven and La Barre.

Moreover, the humanitarian impulse that inspired much Enlightenment thought was not limited to Europe but often extended to distant lands. Montesquieu attacked the enslavement of Negroes in North America and the *Encyclopaedia* also condemned slavery as a violation of human freedom, while the abbé Raynal's *Philosophical and Political History of the Two Indias* [Asia and America], to which Diderot also contributed, protested vehemently against the cruel exploitation of native populations by European colonisers; the work was widely read in the years preceding the French Revolution and went through no fewer than thirty editions.

In spite of the pervasive influence of Locke and Newton and the rapid dissemination of a pragmatic approach to philosophical and scientific problems, the rationalistic Cartesian spirit was too powerful to be ignored, even by those who often seemed to be its fiercest critics. The rejection of Descartes's metaphysical system did not necessarily mean the elimination of the kind of intellectual model on which it rested. Whatever their differences on specific scientific issues, both Descartes and Newton accepted a mechanistic view of the physical world, with its emphasis on the laws of cause and effect. More significantly still, Descartes's insistence on the universality of reason and the need for a correct intellectual method in the search for truth was to have a strong attraction for most eighteenth-century thinkers. Sceptical about the possibility of penetrating the ultimate mystery of nature, whether human or non-human, the *philosophes* were none the less convinced that reality could be analysed by means of fixed universal concepts. This was particularly true not only of the external world but also of human existence. Rejecting the Christian view of man, they still believed that it was possible to speak meaningfully about his 'nature' and to identify a permanent essence which would serve as a true basis for a new philosophy of human existence. They agreed that many recent discoveries and revelations about other lands and cultures radically modified the narrow traditional Christian conception and that it was necessary to allow an important place to relativist factors (such as climate, environment, psychology and the rest), but in the end it still remained possible — and desirable — to speak about 'man'. However divergent their interpretations of human nature might be, most thinkers believed that with care and patience — and of course the right degree of 'enlightenment' — they would be able to produce a coherent and stable description of man's being.

The criticism of religious traditions in the name of history and science, already begun by Bayle and Fontenelle, was to be taken up by later writers, of whom Voltaire was perhaps the most outstanding. Mention has already been made of his *Philosophical Letters* (1734), which were not simply an eulogistic account of the liberalism of English culture and social and political institutions but an ironical attack upon the intolerance and rigidity of religion and society in France. Admittedly, Voltaire's contemporary reputation rested mainly on his tragedies in the classical manner, but his many-sided genius expressed itself in other domains. The *History of Charles XII* (1731), his first serious historical study, was followed by the more ambitious *Age of Louis XIV* in 1751 and the yet vaster *Essay on the Manners and Spirit of Nations* (1769), which sought to give an account of world history. Voltaire's view of the subject led him beyond the lives of kings and statesmen towards the wider cultural history of mankind. In spite of his strong anti-clerical bias, he sought to examine the development of human life by using a historical method that was more philosophical than the theologically-inspired *Discourse on Universal History* of Bishop Bossuet.

By 1750, Voltaire's illustrious contemporary Montesquieu had produced all his major works. An early novel, the *Persian Letters* of 1721, had used the observations of two Persian visitors to France as a means of satirising French religion and society. Like Voltaire, Montesquieu also showed an early interest in history and his *Considerations on the Greatness and Decadence of the Romans* (1734) examined the deeper causes of the rise and fall of the Republic and Empire. Although he was more more interested in the spirit of Roman history than in its particular economic and social aspects, he tried to examine it objectively and, with Voltaire, he can justly claim to be one of the first 'scientific' historians; both rejected the theological interpretation of history as the work of Providence. More important than Montesquieu's early works was the famous *Spirit of the Laws* which appeared in 1748. Based on the assumption that human laws result from the 'nature of things', this vast sprawling treatise explored the impact of physical and historical factors on forms of government, national character and social and political customs; it stressed in particular the formative influence of climate. The whole work is a remarkable example of a sustained attempt to apply explanatory causal principles to a wide range of human phenomena. Equally noteworthy is the moral fervour animating a great deal of the treatise. While accounting for the different kinds of government in physical, historical and psychological terms, Montesquieu cannot conceal his hatred of despotism and his warm attachment to freedom. His humanitarian outlook makes him critical of such evils as religious intolerance, the barbarity of the penal code, and slavery. In spite of his scientific and philosophical attitude, he is compelled to admit that his heart is sometimes at odds with his mind and that his feelings rebel against the principles accepted by his intellect.

Locke's semi-psychological approach to the origin of ideas — together with Newton's demonstration of the power of a fruitful hypothesis based on precise calculation and

9

experiment — inspired Condillac's *Essay on the Origin of Human Knowledge* (1746) which tries to prove that the principle of sensation can be effectively used to account for all the main activities of the human mind. This is possible, he asserts, because sensation 'represents' the external objects by which it is determined. This obviously Lockean aspect of the work is developed in a more original way when Condillac (unlike Locke) refuses to grant any privileged status to voluntary reflection which, he insists, must be rooted, like all mental activities, in sensation. He ingeniously bridges the gap between thought and sensation by stressing the role of language. In this respect Condillac draws on the thought of his day, for several thinkers (including William Warburton, the author of *The Divine Legation of Moses*, part of which had been translated into French in 1744 under the title of *Essai sur les hiéroglyphes des Egyptiens*) were beginning to reject the Cartesian link between language and reason in favour of an emphasis upon its affective origins. Condillac was subsequently diverted from following up this interesting aspect of his thought by a desire to refute Berkeley's idealism and the problem it raised about the existence of the external world; the *Treatise on Sensations* of 1754 tried to overcome the difficulties of idealism by showing how knowledge of the world could be derived from the evidence of sensations. Yet Condillac's exclusive emphasis on sensation betrayed a rigid *a priori* view of mental activity which owed almost as much to the rationalist spirit as to the work of Locke and Newton.

In 1748 Buffon had issued the prospectus of his *Natural History*, a work that was to run to forty-four volumes, the first three of which, devoted to the *Theory of the Earth*, were published in 1749. Although Buffon always remained somewhat apart from the *philosophes*, his scientific activities, like theirs, were closely connected with an overriding interest in 'the great operations of nature'. In spite of his desire to establish an exact scientific method (he recognized that each science must have its own particular method) and his remarkable contributions to the study of natural history, he was inclined to develop broad theories, proclaiming his admiration for 'the great views of an ardent genius who takes in everything at a glance'. Although he came to recognize the importance of variations in the natural species, his unshakeable belief in the unchanging aspects of nature prevented him from developing his ideas in a specifically Darwinian and evolutionary direction. Any far-reaching use of the principle of evolution was also restricted by his insistence that man should be given pride of place in the universe. Man, he affirmed, is 'the only living being whose nature is strong, extensive and flexible enough to adapt itself to the influences of all the climates of the earth'.

Although Rousseau was indebted in varying degrees to all the thinkers so far mentioned, it would be misleading to confine the new 'philosophical spirit' to the major thinkers of the period, for it formed part of a widespread outlook affecting different aspects of Enlightenment culture. Many writers, today forgotten, contributed to the most ambitious and characteristic intellectual enterprise of the century, the publication of the *Encyclopaedia*, of which the energetic and versatile Diderot was the editor-in-chief. Apart from Diderot and, to a lesser extent, d'Alembert, the main *philosophes* contributed comparatively little to this vast work. After writing a number of articles on literary subjects, Voltaire became convinced that this huge encyclopaedia was too cumbersome to become an effective instrument of 'philosophical' propaganda; Montesquieu declined an invitation to write articles on 'Despotism' and 'Democracy', offering instead one on 'Taste', which was left unfinished at his death in 1755. Buffon promised to write on 'Nature' but the article was never published. Rousseau — at a time when he was still unknown — contributed articles on music and wrote only one other major article, 'Political Economy'. On the other hand, Montesquieu and Buffon were frequently quoted in the work itself and d'Alembert, in an eulogy which served as a preface to the fifth volume, hailed the President as a supporter of the enterprise. Moreover, the spirit sustaining the whole work was largely inspired by the principles of the *esprit philosophique*: a criticism of traditional metaphysical and religious absolutes, a marked predilection for nature at the expense of the supernatural, an admiration for science and reason and a fervent humanitarianism which protested against various forms of injustice. Although it was politically conservative, the *Encyclopaedia* was to become a

11

powerful vehicle for the extension of the philosophical spirit of the Enlightenment.

If the new spirit often concerned itself with the removal of what it considered to be irrational and inhuman prejudices and abuses, it also sought to grapple with the main problem created by the rejection of the old absolutes — the nature of man. Man, it was generally agreed, formed part of 'nature' in the widest sense and had the right to search for earthly happiness, but as Rousseau himself asked: 'Where is happiness to be found? Who knows it? Everyone is looking for it, but nobody finds it' (III, 349). Although many thinkers refused to share such doubts, they agreed that it was difficult to produce a universally acceptable solution to the problem. They recognized that the analysis of human nature presupposed a knowledge of 'nature' in general and that without this broader philosophical principle it would be difficult to discuss the moral and social aspects of man's existence. Throughout the century constant efforts were being made to discover a single interpretative principle (rather similar, as we have seen, to the Newtonian principle of gravitation) which would enable thinkers to present a consistent and unified portrait of man's essential being.

Yet this philosophical search for the main characteristics of human nature was being carried out at a time of rapidly broadening cultural horizons. Although thinkers still held fast to the traditional idea that there was a permanent human essence which could be discovered by careful analysis, they were becoming increasingly aware of the importance and diversity of foreign cultures. Whereas French classicism had been somewhat inward-looking as far as the modern world was concerned, believing that artistic perfection had been achieved in antiquity, the Enlightenment eagerly looked beyond national frontiers in order to acquaint itself with the culture of other lands.

Largely ignored during the age of Louis XIV, England was enthusiastically admired in the eighteenth century. Apart from the constant eulogy of Locke and Newton already mentioned, there was great interest in English literature: the so-called 'nature' poets, Thomson and Gray, the novelists Richardson and Fielding, and Shakespeare himself became objects of increasing attention and imitation. English constitutional monarchy was carefully studied by Voltaire and Montesquieu and the traditional idea of the Divine Right of Kings was soon reduced to a mere anachronism. Moreover, readers began to look much further afield as their appetites where whetted by travellers' and missionaries' accounts of distant lands. The Indians of North America or the Chinese were soon to become familiar to readers who wanted to know more about the life and outlook of 'savage' or 'natural' man. The success of Montesquieu's *Persian Letters* in 1721 was at least partly due to their oriental element.

To the *philosophes* this diversity of ideas and customs provided excellent opportunities for attacking the naïvety of those Europeans who considered the religious and moral ideas of their own country to be the epitome of human wisdom. The strongly anti-Christian and anti-clerical current of the time found considerable support in the accounts of simple peoples whose basic humanity often seemed superior to that of the civilised nations of the West. Great play was also made of the relativity of moral ideas, Europeans being condemned for the false assumption that their own ideas were of universal and absolute validity. Nevertheless, relativism had its limits and most *philosophes* hoped to find beneath so many bewildering complexities and contradictions certain basic principles which would allow them to throw light on the true nature of man. Reason could still be used as an instrument for the elaboration of a world of fixed and settled values.

One further fact ought to be mentioned before we consider the reasons for Rousseau's reactions to 'philosophy': the rise of the bourgeoisie and its decisive influence on the new culture. It would be erroneous to see the bourgeoisie as a single homogeneous class, for its particular status varied from one country to another: in France it was an increasingly prosperous social class, made up of professional men, merchants and financiers who were growing resentful at their inferior status in a society still dominated by old aristocratic and ecclesiastical privileges; the new bourgeois believed they were contributing to the economic well-being of the nation while being prevented from actively participating in its social and political life. The exclusion of the bourgeoisie from power and

13

the refusal to modify the traditional class structure are now considered to have been one of the determining causes of the French Revolution. In England, on the other hand, as Voltaire had stressed in the *Philosophical Letters*, the middle classes were treated as useful and worthy members of the community, esteemed and rewarded for the economic benefits they brought to the nation. In a Germany still divided into a multiplicity of states, the middle classes were culturally and socially isolated. If the political aspirations of the bourgeoisie were often frustrated, there can be little doubt about their increasingly important role in cultural life. Although all the *philosophes* were not of bourgeois origin (Montesquieu and Buffon were aristocrat, for example), they tended to write for a middle-class audience. This meant a rapid expansion of a reading public that was anxious to know about new cultural developments, and it is likely that, without these new readers, an enterprise such as the *Encyclopaedia* could never have been commercially viable. The extension of bourgeois influence is also discernible in such *salons* as those of Mme Geoffrin and Mlle de Lespinasse which the *philosophes* regarded as important for the discussion and dissemination of their ideas.

When Rousseau arrived in Paris in 1742 to seek fame and fortune, he differed in many ways from the ambitious young writers with whom he was soon to be associated; in spite of certain common interests and some sympathy for their ideas, his attitude towards the new 'philosophical spirit' was never the same as theirs. In the first place, his Genevan origins meant that from his earliest years he had been imbued with the moral seriousness of his Protestant environment and a deep respect for religious principles which, in spite of periods of backsliding and neglect, he never completely abandoned. Moreover, he had received no formal education; his mother having died a few days after his birth, he was brought up for a short time by his unstable father — a clockmaker who had left Geneva for a time to seek success in Constantinople. He taught his son to read, and prematurely introduced him to sentimental French novels of the seventeenth century and to the heroic moral idealism of Plutarch, thus imbuing him with two contradictory attitudes which were never completely reconciled. When his quarrelsome temperament forced Isaac Rousseau to leave

Geneva, his young son was entrusted first to relatives and then to a Protestant minister living in the country near Geneva. Finally apprenticed to a brutal engraver, Jean-Jacques, at the age of sixteen, decided to leave Geneva. He was immediately converted to Roman Catholicism and then befriended by Mme de Warens, with whom he lived for several years. It was during his sojourn with her that he was given some musical training. More important were his earnest efforts to educate himself. He proposed to build a 'storehouse of ideas' which would make him 'self-sufficient'. His attitude towards knowledge, therefore, was never the same as that of the *philosophes* who, having been brought up in religious schools, either Jesuit or Jansenist, had been provided with the formal literary means of attacking their childhood beliefs. Moreover, Rousseau never had any genuinely disinterested intellectual curiosity and, unlike Diderot, he would rarely entertain ideas for their own sake or explore their purely intellectual implications. The *Confessions* make it clear that the young Rousseau was also intent on furnishing his mind with ideas which would sustain him in his future career, whatever that might be, but he was aware of the difficulties confronting him. 'If there is some advantage in studying alone,' he wrote, 'there are also great drawbacks and especially unbelievable trouble.' It is significant that at this period he resolved to make one particular book his guide: this was Father Bernard Lamy's *Conversations on the Sciences* (1684), an introduction to science which reconciled it with religious principles: all his life Rousseau believed that the value of knowledge was determined by its bearing on man's true 'interest'.

All of this meant that, however closely involved he became with his new environment, Rousseau always remained an 'outsider'. Attracted in some ways by the cultural brilliance and excitement of Paris, he felt that it ran counter to some of his most deeply held convictions. In addition to the influence of early environmental factors, Rousseau also had to reckon with certain distinctive features of his own character, especially his highly developed sensitivity which had been exacerbated by his erratic upbringing and by the lack of early emotional security. He found it difficult to establish a stable balanced relationship with others and his reactions to them

15

were invariably bound up with the complexities of his own inner life. The thwarting of intense emotions could lead to moods of brooding resentment. Still more important was the effect of this sensitivity upon his attitude towards personal fulfilment. Ever impatient of obstacles, he strove for an immediate and complete satisfaction of his desires. As he often said, he was never drawn by 'distant prospects'. A small pleasure within his immediate grasp was always preferred to some future enjoyment, however exalted it might be.

This preoccupation with present satisfaction was bound up with another aspect of his character to which he often referred — a child-like quality which he was never able to suppress. 'Although born a man in certain respects, for a long time I was a child and still am in many others' (I, 235). Referring to an early childhood experience, he observed: 'On this point as on many others, I shall remain a child until my death'. This trait is no doubt connected with what many critics have seen as the 'primitivist' or 'romantic' side of his personality. As a thinker he did not proceed by a slow and arduous chain of reasoning but derived his basic principles from what he believed to be a direct insight into truth — an intuitive apprehension suddenly springing from the depths of his inner being and illuminating a whole area of experience with a dazzling clarity.

The nature of Rousseau's attitude towards philosophical problems emerges very clearly from his three accounts of the inspiration of his first work — the *Discourse on the Arts and Sciences*. When, in October 1749, he was making his way to the Château of Vincennes where his friend Diderot had been imprisoned for having written the allegedly materialistic *Letter on the Blind*, Rousseau happened to notice in a copy of the *Mercure de France* he was carrying that the Academy of Dijon was offering a prize for the best essay on the question: 'Has the re-establishment of the arts and sciences contributed to the purification of morals?' The sight of this question threw him into 'a state of agitation that was close to delirium'; he was overwhelmed by a 'sudden inspiration' which 'dazzled his mind with countless lights' and made him feel a 'giddiness that was close to intoxication'. He thus became an author 'almost in spite of himself' as he 'saw another universe and became

16

another man' and entered 'another intellectual world whose simple, proud harmony he could not envisage without enthusiasm' (I, 416, 1135).

The 'ectasy', 'fever' and 'intoxication' of the experience convinced him that he had been vouchsafed a unique vision of things. Drawn from his most innermost being, this inspiration could not be reconciled with the outlook of contemporary thinkers whose values were those of existing society. This writer who, in his own words, 'became another and ceased to be himself' would henceforth see himself as a being apart; 'vulgar souls' would discern only the superficial aspects of his work whilst 'those who dwelt in the ethereal regions would recognize in him one of their own' (I, 829).

At first Rousseau's awareness of the defects of the old world was perhaps more vivid that his reaction to the beauties of the new 'golden age', for the first *Discourse* itself contained an incisive criticism of the present order while leaving rather vague the precise nature of the one that was to replace it. Yet it is interesting to note that his first reaction was a directly personal one, for he relates how he immediately scribbled down the 'prosopopeia of Fabricius' which was to form part of the final essay. His initial step was to identify himself imaginatively with a historical character — a Roman general — who had denounced the moral shortcomings of his fellow-citizens. In other words, his personal inspiration did not exclude subsequent efforts to express it in conventional historical, philosophical and literary terms. The rhetoric in which the message of this first work is couched owes a great deal to a long-standing literary tradition.

Compared with Rousseau's autobiographical account of the origins of the first *Discourse*, the view of philosophy actually elaborated in the essay may seem rather superficial, but it provides some useful pointers to his later attitude and helps to explain his repudiation of the title 'philosopher'. One reason for the somewhat vague conception of philosophy in this early work is Rousseau's reluctance to separate it from the corruption which he attributes to society as a whole. Modern man has inherited a situation noteworthy for cultural brilliance and moral decadence. Philosophy itself has been inevitably affected by evils influencing other aspects of contemporary life, and

Rousseau makes some effort to explain its particular weaknesses by a brief consideration of its origins and objectives. In general, philosophy, he affirms, has pandered to the current preoccupation with outward appearance at the expense of inner reality. 'How pleasant it would be to live among us, if the outward countenance reflected the state of the heart; if decorum were virtue; if our maxims served as rules of conduct; if true philosophy were inseparable from the title of philosopher!' (III, 7). Rousseau draws the depressing conclusion that the fine apparel with which modern man adorns himself simply conceals his inner ugliness; human nature no longer dares to show itself as it is. The urbane but artificial language used by contemporary writers, though originating in the 'enlightenment of the age', has been transformed into an instrument of 'vain curiosity' and, at worst, of immorality and error.

Rousseau tries to justify his condemnation of existing values by a sweeping assertion about the origins of culture which he attributes to idleness and vice! The study of philosophy, which he tends to identify with metaphysics and science, is dismissed as a purely sterile occupation: born in idleness, it leads to nothing useful. 'Tell me then, illustrious philosophers; you through whom we know in what ratios bodies are attracted to one another *in vacuo*; what are, in the revolution of the planets, the relations of the spaces traversed in equal time; what curves have conjugate points, points of inflexion and retrogression; how man sees everything in God; how soul and body correspond without communication, like two clocks; what stars may be inhabited, what insects reproduce in an extraordinary manner? Answer me, I say, you from whom we have received so much sublime knowledge; even though you had never taught us anything about these matters, should we on that account be less numerous, less well governed, less redoubtable, less flourishing or more perverse?' (III, 18). Rousseau clearly takes a very broad view of philosophy, in which he includes metaphysicians like Malebranche and Leibniz and scientists such as Newton and Réaumur.

When it is not useless, philosophy can be actually harmful. 'Vain and futile declaimers' are animated by false pride and a 'passion to be distinguished from others' which has made them 'degrade and destroy all that is sacred among men'. Rousseau concedes that, although they are not always inspired by a definite hatred of virtue and religion, modern thinkers have allowed themselves to pursue the false objectives offered to them by a corrupt and materialistic society. Whereas ancient statesmen were always talking about morality and virtue, ours speak of nothing but 'commerce and money'. Contemporary culture is therefore sustained by a love of luxury which vitiates it at its very source, weakening the 'vigour of soul' which lends value to all genuine human endeavour. Towards the end of his discourse Rousseau again asks: 'What is philosophy? What do the writings of the best known philosophers contain? What are the lessons of these friends of wisdom? Judging by what they say, should we not take them for a crowd of charlatans, each shouting in a public square, "Come to me, I alone am not a deceiver." One claims that there is no body and that everything is in representation; the other that there is no other substance than matter or any other God than the world. One maintains that there are neither vices nor virtues and that moral good and evil are chimeras; another that men are wolves and can devour one another with an easy conscience. O great philosophers! why do you not reserve these profitable lessons for your friends and your children? You would soon receive your reward and we should not fear to find one of your followers among our own' (III, 27).

Such a diatribe is obviously aimed at a supporter of philosophical idealism such as Berkeley as well as at certain modern materialists (perhaps d'Holbach and La Mettrie), while the next paragraph speaks disparagingly of the 'dangerous reveries of Hobbes and Spinoza'. It is clear from the general tenor of the essay and its conclusions that Rousseau sees himself as the champion of moral values against the insidiously corrupting influence of modern culture. Whereas philosophy is considered to be needlessly complex and artificial, Rousseau praises 'virtue' as the 'science of simple souls', with its principles indelibly 'engraved in the human heart' and readily accessible to anyone who wants to know them. To understand virtue a man needs to do no more than 'withdraw into himself and listen to the voice of conscience in the silence of the passions'. Moreover, moral values do not have to be elaborated with a fine show of words, for they are made real through action, and Rousseau ends his essay by speaking of two great peoples (of Athens and Sparta), 'one of whom knew how to speak well and the other to act well'.

Yet this opposition between philosophy and virtue is not quite absolute, for Rousseau insists on distinguishing the second-rate aspirants to philosophical glory, whose time and energy could be more profitably directed upon useful social tasks, from the great geniuses, Bacon, Descartes and Newton, who are described as 'true preceptors of the human race'. These exalted figures, insists Rousseau, needed no tutors and it is only such outstanding individuals who can justifiably devote themselves to the study of the sciences and the arts. They will never be numerous, for few men can 'raise monuments to the glory of the human mind'. Moreover, only when such thinkers are admitted to the counsels of kings and their 'enlightenment and wisdom' are united with the 'power of princes' will it be possible to combine 'virtue, knowledge and authority' and produce a noble emulation which will contribute to 'the happiness of the human race' (III, 30).

Rousseau's reference to the importance of exceptional genius leads him to mention another theme which, though not inconsistent with the idea of 'virtue' so prominent in the rest of the *Discourse*, is to have much deeper significance for his philosophy as a whole. This is the idea of 'nature'. 'There was no need of masters,' he affirms, 'for those whom nature intended to make its disciples.' Whereas virtue clearly has a fairly narrow moral human meaning, nature is a force animating the whole creation; it is immediate and spontaneous in its expression and has no need of reflection and, unlike virtue, does not require the cooperation of the will.

The idea of nature in the first *Discourse* is too limited for Rousseau to make it the basis of his conception of philosophy. It is by implication what is contrary to existing society, but, as yet, its positive attributes are not clearly envisaged or defined. However, an interesting glimpse of Rousseau's later attitude is indicated at the end of discussion about the corruption of contemporary taste when he writes:

'One cannot reflect on morals without taking pleasure in recalling the image of the simplicity of early times. It is a fine shore adorned only by nature's hands, towards which our eyes are constantly turned and from which we feel ourselves to be going away with regret' (III, 22).

This glimpse of a simpler, purer and more innocent world was one to which Rousseau would frequently return. For the moment, however, he was more eager to denounce contemporary corruption than to suggest specific ways by which the enlightened thinker might remedy it. Nevertheless, it is already apparent that true philosophy must find its inspiration outside the present order of things and, as Rousseau suggests at the very end of his essay, it must begin by reconsidering the reality of man's inner life.

2. The Return to Origins

The view of philosophy elaborated by the self-taught Rousseau in his first work may not seem either profound or original, perhaps because of a refusal to separate it from his condemnation of society as a whole. Since modern society has led to grave moral deterioration and cultural brilliance has become a sign of inner corruption, philosophy has inevitably been affected by the development of outward appearance at the expense of inner worth. With the fine apparel of modern culture being merely 'a base adornment' concealing great ugliness, and human nature no longer daring to show itself as it really is, Rousseau believes that the genuine thinker's first task must be to free himself from the oppressive influence of his immediate environment and, in this respect, his position is no different from that of any man who wishes to find his own true being. Yet, whereas others can concentrate on 'doing well' rather than on 'speaking well', the philosopher must make an effort to rediscover his true vocation. He must begin his search for truth by withdrawing into his own inner self. Rousseau himself forcefully made this point in later years when he wrote in his *Dialogues*: 'Whence could the painter and apologist of nature, which is today so disfigured and calumnied, have drawn his model save from his own heart?' (I, 936). In *Emile*, too, he stressed the importance of 'again becoming ourselves, of concentrating ourselves within ourselves and of circumscribing our soul within the same limits as nature has given to our being' (IV, 112). From his very first work onwards, Rousseau constantly emphasises the importance of 'withdrawing' into oneself as a means of discovering fundamental philosophical principles.

In spite of this need to rediscover his own true being, the thinker's ultimate objective is not to retreat into some merely selfish or subjective form of escape from social corruption but to use his inner life as a means of reaching the true meaning of

22

'nature'. He obviously needs to rely on personal intuition in order to gain insights which are available from no other source, but this is only one step in the elucidation of a reality greater than his own. Within himself he finds not only his own individual reality but that of 'man' himself. Eventually, no doubt, human existence will have to be related to 'nature' in some wider and more objective sense, but the thinker has to begin with the immediate reality of personal existence.

Rousseau realized that it was not an easy task to distinguish between what he describes in *Emile* as 'man's man' and 'nature's man' (IV, 549). If Rousseau saw himself as the 'painter and apologist of nature', he also pointed out that he was 'the historian of the human heart' and that his mission was to trace its 'natural progress'. In order to rediscover 'nature', it was necessary to go back to its primitive forms and to retrace its subsequent development. Rousseau was given an opportunity of doing this when, in 1755, he decided to submit an essay for another prize offered by the Academy of Dijon. The title of the second prize-essay, 'What is the origin of inequality among men and is it authorised by natural law?' invited competitors to deal with a difficult problem, for the question of 'natural law' had been the object of considerable controversy since the seventeenth century. Rousseau himself admits the complexity of the issue in the very first sentence of his preface when he affirms that the Delphic inscription 'Know thyself' is more important than 'all the moralists' big books'. Any proper understanding of the problem of inequality inevitably involves a discussion of the still deeper question of human nature and this, in turn, is bound up with the yet wider issue of 'nature' in general. How can we separate the 'original' aspect of man's being from the accretions and distortions brought about by historical development? In any case, Rousseau insists that the real issue is a philosophical and not a merely historical one, since any effort to describe man's true nature does not mean simply going back to his primitive beginnings but distinguishing between the authentic elements of his being and the artificial characteristics imposed on it by modern society. It will no doubt be necessary to retrace man's history, if only imaginatively and hypothetically — it will be a matter of examining 'a state that exists no longer, has perhaps

23

not existed at all and probably never will exist' — in order to discover the permanent basis of human nature, not simply as it is, but as it might be.

That Rousseau was concerned with a vision of what might have been and might still be is brought out very clearly by his own account of the composition of the essay:

> 'To meditate this great subject at my ease I made a journey of seven or eight days to Saint-Germain with Thérèse, our hostess, who was a good woman, and one of her woman-friends. I consider this trip to be one of the most pleasant of my life. The weather was fine; these good women looked after all cares and expenditure; Thérèse enjoyed herself with them, and I, without any worries, would come and make merry at meal-times. All the rest of the day, plunged in the forest, I sought and found there the image of the earlier times whose history I was proudly tracing; I made a clean sweep of men's little lies, I dared to lay bare their nature, follow the development of the times and things which have disfigured it, and comparing man's man with natural man, to show in his so-called progress the true source of his wretchedness. My soul, exalted by these sublime contemplations, ascended to the divinity and seeing from there my fellow-men follow the blind road of their prejudices, errors, misfortunes and crimes, I cried out to them in a feeble voice which they could not hear: "You madmen who constantly complain of nature, learn that all your evils come from yourselves"' (I, 388-9).

However personal may have been the inspiration of the second *Discourse*, Rousseau was convinced that he was offering men a glimpse of their true being and destiny: 'O man,' he wrote in his preface, 'from whatever country you may be, whatever may be your opinions, listen: Here is your history, as I believe I have read it, not in the books of your fellow-men who are liars, but in Nature which does not lie ... It is so to speak the life of your species that I am going to describe to you according to the qualities you have received, which your education and habits may have depraved but which they have not been able to destroy' (III, 133).

Yet this personal inspiration does not leave him indifferent to earlier discussions of 'natural right' which he believed to have been largely confused or mistaken. He agrees, however, with the statement of the Genevan jurist Jean-Jacques Burlamaqui (1694-1748) who, with his two books *Principles of Natural Right* (1747) and *Principles of Political Right* (1751), had done much to disseminate the ideas of the School of

Natural Law, that all ideas about natural right are 'relative to the nature of man' (III, 124).[1] Unfortunately there was serious disagreement about the basic assumptions underlying this general concept. The Roman view of natural law included animals as well as men and the Stoics established a link between natural and physical law, whereas modern thinkers restrict the notion to rational and moral beings. The Dutch jurist, Hugo Grotius (1583-1645) author of the well-known treatise *De jure belli et pacis* (1625) — translated into French by Barbeyrac as *Du droit de la guerre et de la paix* — affirms that 'natural right consists of certain principles of right reason' and he makes its validity depend on the conformity of a human action with the requirements of a 'reasonable and sociable nature', such conformity characterising a being 'capable of moral direction and accountable for his actions'. At the same time the fact that natural right can be known only to rational beings does not prevent it from being a universal principle rooted in 'the nature of things'. Other thinkers such as Puffendorf and Locke also bring out the moral and well as the rational aspects of natural right. Ultimately such views tend to give it a religious sanction since it is deemed to form part of an objective order created by God.

To this rational and moral conception of natural right were opposed the totally different and much more pessimistic views of Hobbes and Spinoza. Hobbes made a very clear distinction between 'right' (which he identified with freedom) and law (which he identified with obligation). Freedom, in particular, meant 'that liberty which every man hath to make use of his natural faculties according to right reason'. Now the determining principle of every human existence is, according to Hobbes, the right to self-preservation, so that 'every man as much as in him lies shall endeavour to protect his life and members'. Although the principle of self-preservation had been accepted by the supporters of Natural Right, it did not conflict with their main philosophical notions; with Hobbes and Spinoza, on the other hand, it is given supreme importance. Spinoza, for example, extends this principle to the whole of reality which he believes to be engaged in a sheer struggle for survival; desire and power, not reason, thus become the decisive factors in all forms of existence and every individual has the right to protect himself 'without regard to anything but himself'. Human life consists of a fierce struggle for survival and all men are involved in a jungle-like war of 'all against all'. If they accept the constraints of social or political life, it is mainly as a means of protecting themselves against their own destructive impulses.

The principles of natural law and right thus turned on the question of whether man, in his essential being, was rational and social or dominated by feeling and passion. The hypothesis of 'the state of nature' had long been used in attempts to resolve this question, for thinkers wanted to determine what human nature was like before the advent of organized society. Although such discussions had tended to remain abstract and theoretical, the development of history and science in the eighteenth century convinced some philosophers that the problem might be soluble in empirical or experimental terms. Rousseau refers to this idea in his preface when he asks: 'What experiments would be necessary to succeed in knowing natural man; and what are the means of making these experiments in the midst of society?' (III, 123/4). The suggestion of a colony of young people isolated on a desert island had already been put forward by Locke, and Buffon had been attracted by the same idea. The discovery of a child brought up by bears and of another living in the forests of Hanover, as well as the case of the girl found in woods in France, seemed to offer opportunities for observing the power of 'nature's appetites' and laying bare the 'natural movements of the soul'.[2] Nevertheless, as Rousseau admits, the issue could only be discussed — for the time being at least — in hypothetical terms, even though in the notes appended to his second *Discourse* he often quotes supporting evidence drawn from the works of scientists and travellers.

In his own version of the traditional 'state of nature' Rousseau agrees with Hobbes and Spinoza on one essential point: primitive man is a creature of feeling and sensitivity to whom rational moral principles are quite unknown. To discover a genuine natural law, insists Rousseau, we have to go beyond the intellectual subtleties of civilized life and heed 'the voice of nature' and 'meditate on the first and simplest operations of the human soul'. When this has been done, it will be possible to discern two pre-rational principles: the first is the well-known impulse of self-preservation, whilst the second is an equally important 'natural aversion to seeing the death or suffering of any sensitive creature and especially our fellows' (III, 126). According to Rousseau, self-preservation and natural pity are the only principles necessary for an understanding of natural right and there is no need to invoke the idea of sociability. Later on no doubt, as he points out, this primitive natural law will have to be given a more rational basis when the 'successive developments' of man's being have finally 'stifled nature'.

While agreeing with Hobbes on the affective and instinctive basis of primitive life, Rousseau decisively rejects his idea of a 'war of all against all'. He thinks that Hobbes has mistakenly applied to the state of nature ideas derived from later social history. Nevertheless, it is impossible to make any progress in the matter without 'the serious study of man, his natural faculties and their successive developments'. The idea of development is one that is constantly stressed by Rousseau throughout his work and in this respect he is in agreement with many contemporary thinkers who were adopting the same attitude, not only to man's psychological development but to wider and more objective aspects of physical and human reality.

Since the source of modern man's misfortunes lay in a social environment that had been created by a long historical process, Rousseau's vision presented to him — directly and intuitively — a primordial state of being which, however limited and undeveloped, was completely free of the conflicts and contradictions of contemporary life. To return to origins was to simplify human life and reduce it to an almost non-human level — a life of emotions and instincts devoted to the satisfaction of basic needs, especially food and sex. The history of humanity, therefore, had a simple origin, but this origin had the advantage of allowing man to be himself, albeit in a very primitive way. Contentment and fulfilment are never possible — and Rousseau was deeply aware of this need in his own life too — without a sense of inner unity and harmony. The state of nature is not 'a war of all against all', as Hobbes maintains, but a peaceful, solitary and utimately innocent existence. Admittedly, its animal-like character deprives it of any moral value, for morality can arise only when men are in close contact with one another, and no such relationship is possible or necessary to men who live dispersed in the woods.

While insisting on the affective, non-moral aspects of the 'state of nature', Rousseau also points out that even at this primitive stage man is already very different from the animals, for he possesses two special characteristics which play a decisive role in his later development. Unlike the animal, which is little more than 'an ingenious machine to which nature has given senses for it to wind itself up', man can deliberately cooperate with his physical activities in a way that shows him to be a 'free agent'. 'The one chooses or rejects by instinct and the other by an act of freedom.' This means that the animal cannot deviate from a fixed pattern of behaviour, whereas man can do so, often to his own detriment. The specific difference between human beings and animals, therefore, is not to be found in man's intelligence but in his status as a free agent. Although Descartes had denied intelligence to animals, he is at one with Rousseau in stressing the dualism of human nature and, more particularly, the way in which the 'consciousness of freedom' proves the 'spirituality of the soul'. The laws of physics and mechanics, though perhaps capable of explaining the operation of the senses and the formation of ideas, will never be able to account for man's 'power to will or rather to choose' — a power that is to be found 'only in purely spiritual acts'.

As well as possessing freedom, man has another characteristic which distinguishes him from the animals: his capacity for self-improvement. Whereas the animal soon reaches the limits of possible development, man can go on 'perfecting himself'. Admittedly, this perfectibility entails the possibility of degradation, so that if a man can rise far higher than the animals through the use of this 'distinctive, almost unlimited faculty', he can also fall to a much lower level than theirs. Perfectibility, like freedom, explains his misfortunes as well as his happiness, his errors and vices as well as his achievements and virtues.

In the state of nature, freedom and perfectibility remained merely dormant or, as Rousseau puts it, 'virtual capacities' which would become active only when circumstances forced man to adapt himself to a new situation. At first the state of nature was peaceful and unchanging, a static mode of existence in which primitive man effortlessly identified himself with the immediate present: 'his soul which nothing disturbs, gives itself to the sole feeling of its present existence, without any idea of the future' (III, 144). This, for Rousseau, was the fascinating aspect of this state: men did not regret the past or worry about the future; they were content to be themselves in the immediate present, accepting both life and death as part of nature's scheme.

Rousseau's detailed description of the state of nature as a time of primordial innocence is probably connected with his desire to throw into relief the evil and corruption of modern life. In his first *Discourse* he had been content to contrast the defects of contemporary society with the stern demands of true virtue by invoking the historical examples of communities, both ancient and modern, which drew their strength from firm moral principles, but he had taken no more than a rapid glance at these pre-historical times of purity and innocence. In his second work, however, this primitivist element is given a prominent place in the argument which is vigorously opposed to present-day attitudes. Whereas the savage is not moved by his imagination or his heart and asks for nothing more than the satisfaction of his immediate needs, modern man is constantly tormented by problems that leave him inwardly divided and unhappy; never content to be what he is, he is ever seeking to be 'outside himself'. Although the primitive creatures living dispersed in the forests were not yet true men — and it would certainly not be possible or desirable to return to this early condition — the ideal of fidelity to immediate reality, at whatever stage of existence it may be found, offers a lesson which the modern world ought to heed.

Rousseau calls attention to modern man's permanent anxiety over illness and death. Because their healthy constitution protected them from the ills which afflict us today, primitive men were content to accept nature's laws and, when the time came, 'they died without anyone noticing that they ceased to exist, and almost without noticing it themselves' (III, 137). Not for them the desperate, though futile, recourse to medicine as a means of saving people from the consequences of their own unhealthy habits! Similarly, primitive man knows nothing of 'the ardent impetuous passion which makes one sex necessary to the other, the terrible passion which defies all dangers, overthrows all obstacles and, in its fury, seems suited to destroy the human race which it is meant to preserve' (III, 157). Sexual feeling has been diverted from its true function by the pressure of social habits, one consequence of which has been to encourage women to dominate the men they ought to obey! Modern love is based on complex notions and sentiments, including jealousy and vanity, which originate in men's constant need to compare themselves with one another. Such an attitude, insists Rousseau, is unknown to primitive man who can satisfy his simple physical desires 'calmly and almost without effort'. 'The imagination which makes so many ravages among us does not speak to savage hearts; each one peacefully awaits nature's impulse, gives way to it indiscriminately and with more pleasure than fury and, when need has been satisfied, all desire is extinguished' (III, 158).

When men finally left the state of nature — perhaps because of a sudden change in their physical environment — their dormant attributes began to develop; rudimentary relationships with other human beings gradually formed, together with 'some kind of reflection'. A decisive stage was reached with 'the establishment and distinction of families' and the introduction of a 'kind of property'. This constituted the first social revolution and the emergence of a simple form of communal life. This change was not free from certain dangers, for the individual now began 'to look at himself and compare himself with others', so that he was henceforth exposed to the insidious influence of pride and envy. Yet the advantages of this new stage of human existence outweighed the disadvantages, for it was possible to enjoy 'the sweetest feelings known to men — conjugal and paternal love'. Man had not yet lost his natural freedom and he was still satisfied with simple needs. This was probably the happiest period of his history: 'being placed by nature half-way between the stupidity of the brutes and the fatal enlightenment of civil man, and limited equally by instinct and reason to protect himself from the evil which threatens him, he is restrained by natural pity from doing harm to anyone, and is not impelled to it, even after

30

receiving harm' (III, 170). This phase of human history, by keeping 'a just balance between the indolence of the primitive state and the lively activity of our pride, must have been the happiest and most durable period'. A particularly striking feature of this mode of life was the combination of self-sufficiency with the pleasures of 'independent intercourse'.

This simple social life came to an end with the discovery of agriculture and metallurgy, which immediately led to a division of labour and the establishment of property, with its disastrous distinction between 'mine' and 'thine'. 'The first man who, having enclosed a piece of land, thought of saying "this is mine" and found people simple enough to believe him, was the true founder of civil society' (III, 164). People who had hitherto lived peacefully together became involved in rivalry and conflict. With the development of memory, imagination and reason, life became complicated and unstable; inequalities which had been unimportant in the state of nature began to play a dominant role in social life. The distinction between 'appearance' and 'being', which Rousseau had already attributed to modern society in the earlier *Discourse*, became a permanent feature of human existence: 'it was necessary for people to show themselves to be other than what they really were'. Being and appearing became two different things, and from this distinction emerged 'imposing ostentation, deceitful cunning and all the vices which follow in their train' (III, 174). Freedom gave way to slavery; people were divided into rich and poor, powerful and weak, as all were filled with the ' dark inclination to do themselves mutual harm' and achieve their own profit at another's expense. Society was finally transformed into the 'war of all against all' which Hobbes had mistakenly attributed to the 'state of nature'. The rich preyed upon the poor like 'hungry wolves who, having once tasted human flesh, will be satisfied with no other food'. Thus men became 'greedy, ambitious and wicked' as they struggled to survive in the most horrible state of war. A point having been reached when even the rich and powerful could no longer feel secure, they devised 'the most carefully conceived plan that ever entered the human mind': they suggested the establishment of a supreme power which would govern men according to agreed laws and would 'defend and protect all members of the association, repulse common enemies, and maintain them in eternal concord'. The cleverness of this idea is revealed by the way in which power based on mere force was changed into a legal right supported by universal consent. In fact, the founding of political society was a confidence-trick perpetrated by the rich at the expense of the poor who 'hastened to put on their chains in the belief that they were assuring their freedom'. Property and inequality were at last given legal sanction. 'For the profit of a few ambitious men' the whole human race was subjected to 'toil, servitude, and misery' (III, 176-8).

The establishment of organized society was a decisive stage in human development and in this respect Rousseau makes use of yet another traditional concept — the social contract. Like the thinkers of the School of Natural Law, he stresses the idea that the establishment of organized society was due to a rational choice. However mistaken men may have been about the consequences of their action, they were undoubtedly taking a step which was intended to be to their advantage. Society did not come about by some natural process but was the result of a deliberate choice. Unfortunately the weaker and poorer members of the community failed to see that this new society would simply perpetuate the immediate situation by confirming the superiority of the powerful. As a fuller discussion of the social contract will also involve reference to Rousseau's later writings, it will be enough to stress here its decisive historical role in the development of political society which radically changed not only man's way of life but his very character.

Social and political inequality was consolidated and extended by subsequent developments — by the formation of a magistrature that divided the state into powerful and weak and, finally, by the change from legitimate to arbitrary power which reduced all members of the community to the position of master and slaves. This last stage of inequality is sheer despotism which in a sense brings about a new but quite artificial and corrupt 'state of nature' by making all men equal in their servitude. With the advent of despotism, the social process has come full circle and the social contract is abolished since society now rests on force alone: oppressors and rebels cannot complain of injustice, but only of 'imprudence or misfortune', all right having been completely destroyed.

At the end of his *Discourse* Rousseau points out that his account of the establishment and history of society has been 'deduced from man's nature by the sole light of reason' and owes nothing to 'sacred dogmas'. He has shown, he affirms, that inequality barely exists in the state of nature where physical differences do not constitute a problem, but, becoming increasingly important with the development of 'our powers and the progress of the human mind', it is made stable and legitimate by the foundation of political society. It follows that 'the moral inequality authorised by positive (i.e. human as opposed to natural) law is contrary to natural right whenever it is not proportionate to physical inequality'. The enormous disparity between the poor and the rich in modern society is as irrational as it is inhuman, for it is contrary to natural law 'for a child to command an old man, an idiot to lead a wise man and a handful of beings to be gorged with superfluities while the hungry multitude lacks the wherewithal to live' (I, 194). The fact that Rousseau's last paragraph owes something to his reading of Montaigne in no way diminishes the eloquence of his forceful protest against social and economic injustice. In this respect, the second *Discourse* marks a decisive advance upon the first, where the criticism of modern society was set against a more remote historical background. Now seen in relation to an extended and carefully elaborated view of human evolution and the gradual development of man's powers, the basic inequality of modern society, with its inevitable conflict between rich and poor, is presented in a more vivid and dramatic light.

Although the second *Discourse* was written while Rousseau was still friendly with the *philosophes* and actively participating in Parisian life, it clearly shows that he was never completely identified with their cause. The inspiration and tone of the work are those of a man who feels himself to be separated from professional writers by his powerful sense of literary vocation. This is very apparent in an eloquent letter, sent on 28 November 1754 to the Genevan clergyman Jean Perdriau, in which he announced his intention of dedicating his *Discourse on Inequality*, without first obtaining official permission, to the

Republic of Geneva. The sentiments expressed in this letter are closely related to the heroic moral principles affirmed in the first *Discourse*. If he decided to honour Geneva by his dedication, it was not, he affirmed, in order to win the favour of a particular group, since he was following the dictates of justice and reason; in this respect, 'the reproaches of the whole universe' would affect him far less than the 'avowal of his conscience'. To the possible objection that no such dedication had ever been made before, he replied that 'in praiseworthy matters it is better to give an example than to receive it' and he believed he had 'too just reasons for being nobody's imitator'. Furthermore, in an age remarkable for its 'pusillanimous circumspection', there was merit in a 'general boldness which, to do good, sometimes shakes the puerile yoke of convention'. Of his own independence he had no doubt. 'Isolated by men, holding to nothing in society, devoid of any kind of pretensions and seeking my happiness itself only in that of others, I believe that I am at least exempt from those social prejudices which make the wisest men bend their judgements to the maxims advantageous to them.' Indifferent to the criticism of particular bodies, he 'yielded only to reason' and he would henceforth be his 'sole censor' because he would be relying on his conscience, 'that incorruptible inner judge which overlooks nothing bad and condemns nothing good, and which never deceives us when we consult it sincerely'. He ends with a bold proclamation of his literary vocation: 'If the detachment of a heart which clings neither to glory nor to fortune, nor even to life can make it worthy of proclaiming the truth, I dare to believe that I am called to this sublime vocation.' If such a calling means that he must live in poverty and independence, he will certainly do so, even though this will not prevent him from being an 'honest, true and zealous citizen' (*CC*, III, 55-60).

The *Confessions* reiterate the same proud sense of vocation. 'I felt that to write in order to have bread would have soon stifled my genius and killed my talent which was less in my pen than in my heart, and born solely from a lofty, proud way of thinking which alone could sustain it. Nothing great and vigorous can come forth from a venal pen. Necessity and perhaps greed would have made me write quickly rather than well. If the need for success had not plunged me into cliques, it would have made me utter not so much useful and true things as things which would please the multitude and, instead of becoming a distinguished author, I should have been only a scribbler. No; no! I have always felt that the author's condition was and could be famous and respectable only in so far as it was not a trade. It is too difficult to think nobly when one is thinking only in order to live. To dare and to be able to utter great truths a man must not depend on success. I cast my books among the public with the certainty of having spoken for the common good and without any concern for the rest' (I, 402-3). This was why, as he told his clergyman-friend Jacob Vernes, his serious, deep works about virtue and freedom were quite different from 'all the frippery of fashionable little philosophy' (*CC*, IV, 116).

Apart from strengthening his sense of vocation, the second *Discourse* also led him to re-establish relations with his native Geneva. Hitherto this had been prevented by his continued adherence to the Roman Catholicism to which he had been converted soon after his departure from Geneva in 1728. The influence of the *philosophes* whom he frequented in Paris had probably been effective enough to detach him from strict orthodoxy and even to dissipate any lingering attachment to specific Christian doctrines. Although he had formed a strong aversion to theological disputes and this 'farrago of petty phrases' with which men obscured the essence of true religion, he was certainly no atheist and the general religious outlook developed during his sojourn with Mme de Warens still persisted. 'The study of man and the universe had everywhere shown me final causes and the intelligence which directed them' (I, 392); he also believed that the Gospel was of universal validity and went beyond the 'base and stupid interpretations' of Jesus Christ's life and character. Moreover, he also accepted the Protestant view that the sovereign had the right to fix the form of the national cult, so that to become a Genevan again meant returning to Protestantism and 'accepting the form of worship established in his country'. When in 1755 he sought re-admission to the Church of Geneva, it was a civic rather than a religious gesture. Even so, he insisted later on that the *philosophes* had 'shaken' rather than overthrown his fundamental

35

religious convictions and he was to see religion as the main issue on which they were irrevocably divided.

In spite of his new-found attachment to Geneva, it was not until 1758 that Rousseau was given an opportunity of linking up his patriotic feelings with the criticism of society and the analysis of human nature begun in the early *Discourses*. Admittedly he had left Paris in 1756 and gone to live in the country where he had carried out a radical material and moral 'reform' which was intended to free him from the insidious influence of the capital, so that he could now take a more detached view of the evils he felt himself called upon to castigate. In 1757 there appeared the fifth volume of the vast *Encyclopédie* which was being edited by Diderot and d'Alembert and for which Jean-Jacques himself had been invited to write articles on music, as well as a substantial article on 'Political Economy'. This fifth volume contained an article on Geneva written by d'Alembert, who had visited the republic the previous year in order to see his friend Voltaire and to gather material for the article. When it was finally published, it contained two suggestions that aroused vigorous protests from the Genevan community. D'Alembert's intention had been to praise the toleration of the Genevan clergy which he no doubt wished to contrast with the intolerance of French Roman Catholicism. Unfortunately, however, he had gone so far as to say that some of the Genevan clergy were so broad-minded that they no longer believed in Christ's divinity. Another and — from Rousseau's point of view — more important point was d'Alembert's suggestion, made no doubt at Voltaire's instigation, that a theatre should be established in Geneva. It was this which prompted Rousseau to write his *Letter to M. d'Alembert on the Theatre (Lettre à M. d'Alembert sur les Spectacles)*.

To the religious question Rousseau devotes only a few somewhat embarrassed pages at the beginning of the *Letter*. The weakening of his links with Christian orthodoxy made him reluctant to become involved in this aspect of the dispute, so that, in spite of the relevance of some of his comments to the development of his religious outlook at this time, they form only a very minor part of the whole work. Even the question of the theatre was not without personal significance. He had always been fond of the theatre and on one occasion — in 1737 — he confessed to having been so deeply moved by a performance of Voltaire's *Alzire* that he was almost physically ill (*CC*, V, 54-7). When he arrived in Paris in 1742, he had with him the manuscript of a play, *Narcisse*, as well as a new system of musical notation through which he hoped to achieve fame and fortune. The play was eventually performed, though without success, and in 1753 he published the text, together with an important preface in which he examined some of the points raised by the controversy around the first *Discourse*. Although his withdrawal from Paris cut him off from its cultural life, it made him still more aware of its shortcomings. This means that the *Letter to d'Alembert* not only denotes a resurgence of Rousseau's patriotism but also continues his criticism of contemporary culture and society by relating it to a specific issue. In the *Confessions* Rousseau points out that the 'gentleness of soul' discernible in the *Letter* was due to the circumstances of its composition, for it was written when he had 'returned to his element' in the countryside where, as he says in the preface to the *Letter*, 'solitude eases the soul and appeases the passions produced by the disorder of society'. Moreover, the work was given a deeply personal significance by Rousseau's belief that he was soon to die; as he indicates at the end of his preface, he expected it to be his last production. He subsequently treated it as his favourite one. 'I love it more than all the others', he told his friend Deleyre in October 1758, 'because it has saved my life and has served as a distraction in moments of grief when, without it, I should have died of despair' (*CC*, V, 160). To a friend of his last years, Dusaulx, he described it as 'his favourite book, his Benjamin'. 'I produced it effortlessly, at the first attempt and in the most lucid moments of my life. Whatever people may do, they will never take away from me, in this respect, the glory of having written a man's work' (*CC*, V, 71).

Whatever its personal significance, the *Letter to d'Alembert* dealt with a controversial issue of long standing.[3] Although the early Church fathers had condemned the theatre as incompatible with Christian morality, the medieval Church had encouraged the performance of 'mysteries' of religious inspiration. The Renaissance and Reformation of the sixteenth century had witnessed a revival of ecclesiastical hostility towards the theatre in France, but it was only in the seventeenth century that a prolonged and serious controversy took place, having been partly provoked by the rivalry between Jesuits and Jansenists, the latter's austere moral views leading them to a severe condemnation of the theatre. In spite of the royal protection at first accorded to the theatre, the ageing Louis XIV eventually came down on the side of severity and Bishop Bossuet produced a powerful polemical piece against the theatre with his influential *Maxims and Reflections on Comedy*, 1694. After the death of Louis XIV, and with the advent of the pleasure-loving Regent, the debate assumed a somewhat different character; moral and social considerations prevailed over religious ones and, with the new importance attached to the 'philosophical spirit' and to the theme of earthly happiness, the theatre found an increasing number of supporters. Helped by the eloquence and vigour of Voltaire and the general approval of the Encyclopaedists, the cause of the theatre seemed to be assured of ultimate triumph, even though there was still strong opposition from those who remained loyal to the strict Christian tradition.

Rousseau removes the debate from the traditional theological context and relates it to the moral principles discussed in his earlier work. The *Letter*, however, has visionary as well as critical aspects which make it both the most lyrical and the most austere of Rousseau's writings — austere when it is putting forward ethical reasons for attacking d'Alembert's suggestion for establishing a theatre in Geneva, and lyrical when it looks forward to the free and joyous entertainments which would befit a regenerated fatherland. The theatre is condemned as a characteristic example of corrupt civilisation and as a grave threat to the moral integrity of a little republic which has so far escaped the pernicious effects of French society. The issue is given yet wider significance when the whole question of entertainment is related to one of the major themes of Rousseau's earlier works: the general problem of human nature. The French theatre is condemned not simply for its possible effects upon Genevan republicanism but also for its harmful repercussions upon the very nature of man himself. Yet at the end of the work the dark claustrophobic atmosphere of the early part gives way to a sunnier, happier and more expansive mood as memory and imagination combine to portray the kind of entertainment suitable for men living in freedom and equality.

The broad basis of Rousseau's position is indicated very clearly at the outset when he invokes the principle of 'nature', and, more speicifically, the nature of man. 'Man's condition', he declares, 'has its pleasures which derive from his nature and spring from his labours, his relations, his needs'[4] (p. 23). The point is reiterated at the end of the work when he says that he would like men 'to draw their pleasures and their duties from their condition and themselves' (p. 184). When it is tested against this fundamental principle, the theatre is found to be wanting in almost every respect. The audience is obliged to adopt an unnatural physical posture, as it sits immobilised and silent in a confined space, each person being passively isolated from his fellow-men as he lets himself become absorbed by the events on the stage. Instead of using their time in a practical way, people thus 'forget themselves' as they become 'occupied with alien objects' (p. 90). There is also something unnatural about the way in which feelings experienced in the theatre are directed away from ourselves, for we 'attach our heart to the stage as though it were ill at ease within us'.

Throughout his essay Rousseau castigates the theatre for its constant 'reversal of natural relationships'. He finds striking proof of this in the prominence accorded to women who, instead of being content with the quiet domestic role for which nature intended them, thrust themselves shamelessly before the public eye. In this respect the theatre merely reproduces a recognized characteristic of social life: in the *salons* women hold sway as the arbiters of taste and fashion, pronouncing judgement on cultural, moral and social matters. Because of their subservience to women, men are forced to lead 'an indolent and cowardly life'. Rousseau offers a satirical portrait of a typical *salon* dominated by a 'female idol' before whom men prostrate themselves in adoration. 'In Paris each woman collects in her rooms a harem of men who are more womanish than she, who know how to pay all kinds of homage to her beauty except the one of which it is worthy — that of the heart. But see these same men, always constrained in these voluntary prisons, get up, sit down again, incessantly go to and from the fireplace and the window, pick up and put down a fan countless times, leaf through books, glance at pictures, turn and pirouette in the room while the idol, lying motionless in her *chaise-longue*, moves only her tongue and her eyes' (p. 136). How different is all this from ancient times when women stayed at home and busied themselves with their domestic duties while their men-folk were working! 'We have fallen in everything.' The indolent way of life imposed on modern man by the domination of women has destroyed his strength and vigour. It is enough, for example, to compare his feeble activities with the amazing physical endurance of Roman soldiers. 'The route, work and burden of the Roman soldier tire us merely to read about them and overwhelm the imagination' (p. 137).

The supremacy of women in modern society is clearly reflected in the main theme of the theatre — love. This 'dangerous passion' is allowed to usurp the place of 'natural simple feelings which no longer move anybody'. Since love represents the 'reign of women', plays devoted to this theme simply help to extend the influence of the female sex; they make 'women and girls the tutors of the public' and give them 'the same power over the audience as they have over their lovers' (p. 73). Once again Rousseau evokes the practice of the Ancients who refused to expose women to public judgement in the belief that they 'honoured their modesty by remaining silent about their other virtues'. In modern society, on the other hand, the woman who enjoys the most esteem is the one who makes most noise and sets the tone so imperiously 'that humble scholars basely beg her favours' (p. 76).

In condemning the theatre so severely Rousseau was probably not unmindful of his own earlier fondness for it. By presenting himself as a defender of 'truth', 'justice', 'humanity' and 'patriotism', he was reacting strongly against his own sensibility: primordial affections were being praised at the expense of debilitating emotions. The priority accorded to emotion in the theatre means that all practical moral consider-ations are subordinated to the principle of pleasure; since the theatre's main object is to please, it will flatter the passions, whatever they may be, of any nation it serves; it will be a docile instrument, not a rigorous master, of emotions which are in direct conflict with the rational and moral activity of the will. Reason and will are useless in a theatre dominated by *la tendresse*; the theatre weakens the will and 'disposes the soul to too tender feelings' (pp. 68-9).

Rousseau also stresses that the psychological effect of the theatre is quite independent of the particular emotions it portrays, for he readily acknowledges that these may be both good and bad. Whatever the specific quality of the emotions described, the theatre will 'make men effeminate', reduce their 'strength and virtue' and lead to indolence and inaction (p. 74). He unhesitatingly rejects the Aristotelian principle of the 'purgation of the passions'. Being completely subservient to the demands of emotion, the theatre can have no moral value, especially in a society which admires only wit and knowledge and despises 'will and modest virtue'.

Since the theatre cannot alter human nature — and this is indeed fortunate when we recall that man was 'born good' — it may be argued that in a corrupt society it will occasionally stimulate 'a remnant of natural feeling'. Yet such virtuous reactions remain purely sterile and quite irrelevant to the practical tasks of daily life where true citizens should be 'active, hard-working and self-reliant'. Rousseau cannot help imvoking the example of the mountain-people (*Les Mont-agnons)* he knew in his childhood; they were self-sufficient and versatile in their talents, living a physically confined and yet a very full and active life. He constantly laments the disappearance of such people from the modern world, for their presence in our midst would help to remind us of our true humanity.

When he examines the theatre in more detail, Rousseau blames tragedy for its remoteness from real life; it presents us with 'abominable monsters', 'atrocious actions' and 'horrors' more characteristic of 'gigantic beings' than of ordinary men. Admittedly, comedy is closer to the everyday world but, in Rousseau's opinion, it presents a distorted view of moral values. Even a great playwright like Molière saw fit to ridicule virtue. In a well-known section of the *Letter* Rousseau describes Alceste, the main character of *Le Misanthrope,* as 'upright, sincere, estimable' and 'a truly good man' whom the dramatist holds up to derision. Elsewhere too Molière 'ridicules goodness and simplicity' and teaches men to despise 'the sacred relationships on which the order of society is based.' According to Rousseau, Alceste is made ridiculous because 'he hates the wickedness of his contemporaries'. To some extent Rousseau is clearly identifying himself with the character, comparing society's treatment of Alceste with his own contemporaries' reaction towards himself. Yet, all questions of moral heroism apart, Rousseau maintains that the theatre does not even respect simple human qualities. Typical of modern comedy is its mockery of 'nature's most sacred rights and most touching feelings' as, for example, when old men are derided by young fops and family obligations flouted by irresponsible children.

Alongside this criticism of the theatre as a form of entertainment that encourages emotion at the expense of virtue, Rousseau attacks the harmful influence of the actors themselves. The profligacy of actors — condemned by many generations of moralists — had been recognized since ancient times and for many years the Church had refused them burial in consecrated ground. While taking up once again this traditional theme, Rousseau goes on to make a more subtle psychological criticism of the actor as such, condemning him not simply for the immorality of his personal life but also for the very activity by which he seeks to justify his existence. Unlike the simplicity of 'true genius' which 'draws its resources from itself' and is content 'to enjoy its own being' without further reflection, the actor's talent is 'to mimic himself, assume another character than his own and appear different from what people are' (p. 106). The actor 'makes traffic of himself in a servile and base manner'. His final degradation is to put himself at the mercy of others and to depend on their reactions for his success or failure.

Everything in the theatre, therefore, denotes artificiality and corruption. No doubt this kind of entertainment may have to be tolerated in a large country like France where its abolition could lead to still greater evils such as crime and brigandage, but its introduction into a comparatively innocent republic like Geneva would merely open the way to degradation and vice. Moreover, Rousseau believes that the situation in Geneva is all the more critical since it is already being exposed to the insidious influence of French culture. If the first part of the *Letter* depicts the modern theatre and its social background in sombre colours, Rousseau devotes the last part to his vision of a regenerated Geneva and the entertainment most suited to it.

To some extent he had prepared the way for this by his eulogy of the ancient Greek theatre, the great merits of which were contrasted with the defects of the modern stage. Although the Romans treated actors as slaves, Rousseau points out that the Greeks held them in such high esteem that they were often assigned important public functions, both at home and abroad. The reasons for this are, according to Rousseau, easy to understand. Since the Greeks were the actual inventors of the theatre, its effects were not yet known, so that actors were not treated with the contempt directed against them by later generations. Moreover, the theatre was an integral part of national life and, as such, was held to be of sacred origin, actors being considered as priests rather than as entertainers, and, while the subjects of their plays were invariably drawn from the nation's past, the actors were esteemed as citizens offering their compatriots 'the history of their country'. The instructive function of these dramatic performances was also related to the Greeks' love of freedom. Furthermore, Rousseau takes pains to remind his readers that all female roles were played by men, so that 'one did not see in their theatre this mingling of men and women which turns ours into so many schools of immorality'. More important still was the absence of all motives inspired by greed and self-interest, this moral elevation being sustained by a refusal to transform the theatres into 'dark prisons'; all performances were in the open air in the presence of nature. 'These great and splendid entertainments, given beneath the sky, in full view of the whole nation, presented on all sides only combats, victories, prizes, objects capable of inspiring the Greeks with eager emulation and warming their hearts with feelings of honour and glory' (p. 105).

When Rousseau turns his attention to Geneva, he imagines it imbued with a 'festal air' originating in the spontaneous enjoyment of communal activity in the midst of nature. Stressing the close link between true entertainment and physical nature and repeating his earlier description of the Greek theatre, Rousseau tells the Genevans that 'it is in the open air, it is beneath the sky that you must gather and abandon yourselves to the sweet feeling of your happiness'. Such pleasures will be without constraint, for they will be as free and generous as the Genevans themselves when 'the sun lights up their innocent entertainments'. Such a bright picture is in striking contrast to the dark pessimism of the earlier account of the theatre and is described in a typical Rousseau image: 'Innocent joy tends to expand in full daylight, but vice is the friend of darkness' (p. 191).

The simplicity and innocence which Rousseau has repeatedly — and with nostalgia — evoked in his previous references to nature are here realised in a specifically national and patriotic setting. At the same time, he sees the whole community participating in a creative form of entertainment. As soon as someone sets up a flower-adorned stake in the middle of a public square, all the citizens will quickly become both actors and spectators as they gather joyfully around it. Instead of the isolation and darkness of the theatre, 'each one will see and love himself in the other' in order that all may be 'the better united' (p. 187). This idea of a close-knit, happy and active community is one that is dear to Rousseau's heart and is here described with lyrical emotion. The tyranny and servility of large cities are replaced by a mood of happy fulfilment.

The personal aspect of Rousseau's evocation is clearly indicated by a reference to his own childhood: he recalls the occasion when he and his father were watching a military dance and observing its effect upon the rest of the citizens. He cannot easily forget those days when the sight of a whole republic enjoying 'peace, freedom, equity and innocence' compelled his father to say to him: 'Jean-Jacques, love your fatherland'. To this personal recollection is added a classical reminiscence: he recalls the pure joy of the naked Lacedaemonian dancers whose 'frugal, hard-working life' and 'pure and severe morals and strength of soul could alone make innocent' an entertainment which would shock any other nation. Modern eyes — even the Genevans' — can no longer bear such a sight, however pure and unsophisticated it may be, but the Lacedaemonian festivals at least remind us of 'the secret charm of patriotism and freedom' and the 'sweet conformity of a happy national life'. May the happy youth of Geneva 'transmit to its descendants the virtue, freedom and peace which it receives from its fathers'! Such is the wish with which Rousseau ends a work intended to defend and enhance the simple merits of his native republic in the face of a grave threat from a large and corrupt neighbouring culture. Only with the help of 'nature' — the nature of man effectively related to a wider physical and social setting — will it be possible to reach this goal.

3. The New Man

As Rousseau himself pointed out, his early work was mainly critical, its intention being to dispel errors and illusions about the society and culture of his day. If much of this criticism involved constant references to 'nature', this was treated principally as a concept intended to show what the modern world was not, rather than what it could — and should — be. With the description of the 'state of nature' in the *Discourse on Inequality* Rousseau returned to the origins of humanity, but he described how subsequent history had led it away from its true goal of genuine fulfilment towards decadence and corruption. Since man had never realized the possibilities of his essential being, it was necessary to complement the critical writings with a sustained and constructive effort to describe his true nature and the society best suited to his needs. So far Rousseau had done no more than give a few glimpses — for example, in the idealised lyrical portrayal of a regenerated Geneva in the *Letter to d'Alembert* — of what a genuine human community could be like. Even the description of Clarens in his novel *La Nouvelle Héloïse* (1761) was merely an example of a small provincial society in an ideal rural setting; it did not attempt to lay down a systematic philosophy of existence or to establish the principles of social and political life.

It was with the publication of *Emile* in 1762 — together with the *Social Contract* — that Rousseau presented a philosophy of man and a serious treatise on political right. Rousseau saw *Emile* as his most important work: 'It will one day make a revolution among men', he declared, 'if ever they recover their sincerity.' While recognizing it as a landmark in the history of educational thought, later generations have often preferred the complex Jean-Jacques of the *Confessions* and *Reveries*, the austere political theorist of *The Social Contract* or even the social critic of the first *Discourse*. The lessons of *Emile* having been assimilated and surpassed by later reformers such as

46

Pestalozzi and Froebel, it remains for many people an unread masterpiece. It has been shown too that many of its ideas were already to be found in liberally-minded predecessors such as Montaigne and Locke. Montaigne, for example, had attacked bookish pedantry, insisting that education should be a pleasant, gradual process which gave proper intention to its physical as well as to its intellectual aspect, while Locke too had opposed mere bookishness and encouraged physical activities.[1] Yet Rousseau's treatise is not only more systematic than their works but is also imbued with an idealistic fervour which lifts it above mere pedagogy and relates it to a vision of fulfilled manhood. Rousseau himself warned his contemporaries against seeing *Emile* as a mere educational manual, for it was a 'philosophical treatise on the nature of man' and, more specifically, 'a treatise on man's natural goodness, intended to show how vice and error, being alien to his constitution, are introduced into it from the outside and gradually change it for the worse' (I, 934).

In the very first sentence Rousseau establishes the essential antithesis on which the work is based: 'Everything is good when it comes forth from God's hands, everything degenerates in man's hands'. The idea of nature's 'goodness' is a constantly recurring theme which stands in sharp contrast to the corruption and evil of contemporary society. From the very outset it is clear that 'nature' involves far more than man's existence, for it is a cosmic principle of divine origin. Yet it is potentially close to man since his own particular nature, when properly understood, is related to this wider context. In the modern world, however, nature serves predominantly as a critical principle, highlighting what man is not, while indicating in an unmistakable way what he might become. If, therefore, 'nature' is opposed to 'society' and 'opinion', it cannot be equated with any immediately accessible historical or social experience but has to be related to a more fundamental conception of reality. To a clear-sighted and inspired observer like Rousseau, nature may present no problem, but his readers (as he recognizes) are still faced with the difficult task of understanding its elusive hidden meaning.

Since the antithesis of nature and society involves more than a simple opposition between two aspects of observable reality,

Rousseau's thought has to move on two different planes: on the one hand, it treats society as a fixed, almost static condition and, on the other, nature as a dynamic principle, a norm and a goal that may ultimately become a part of man's actual experience when he has properly understood its full meaning. In any case, the true significance of nature will appear only gradually and, as Rousseau has already indicated in his hypothetical reconstruction of human history in the *Discourse on Inequality,* it is necessary first of all to go back to its origins, for these will provide a starting-point for the analysis of its subsequent development. The genetic method applicable to the history of humanity is also valid for the development of the individual. Any attempt to explain the authentic origin of human nature must go beyond scientific and historical research and start with an imaginative effort to discover the sources of man's early being. Into this creation of a new man Rousseau has infused a fervour and intensity which lifts his work above the literary sources to which he is sometimes indebted. Although the 'painter of nature' and the 'historian of the human heart' (as he calls himself, I, 928, 936) often finds it difficult to separate his own passionately held convictions from the memory of ideas read in the works of others, the argument of *Emile* derives its momentum from the constant opposition between the corruption of immediate reality and the glowing possibilities of a human existence regenerated by the power of nature.

In *Emile* Rousseau gives up the pseudo-historical method of the *Discourse on Inequality*, which traces man's development from his primitive state to his present corrupt condition, in order to concentrate on the life of a single individual brought up far from the social environment of his day. He seeks to trace the different stages through which such a being would have to pass in order to become a mature man. Rousseau believes that, when it is freed from harmful social influences, nature can provide a clear and consistent guide for the description of such a development. That is why he speaks so often of 'the advance of nature' and constantly urges his readers to follow 'the path of nature'. The stability and coherence of nature being guaranteed by God, human existence can find a clue to its own development in the 'order of nature', or, as Rousseau also puts it, in a 'well-ordered nature'. Having once established man's true origins, it is mainly a question of perceiving the power of his 'primitive dispositions' and of tracing their 'successive developments' (IV, 501).

Emile, therefore, like all the rest of Rousseau's constructive works, places an unbounded confidence in the 'goodness of nature'. 'Let us lay down as an incontrovertible maxim that nature's first movements are always right: there is no original perversity in the human heart: there is not a single vice in it, of which I cannot say how or where it came in' (IV, 322). He was to re-affirm the same point in his polemic with the Archbishop of Paris: 'I have described the way in which the first movements of nature are born and I have followed so to speak their genealogy, and I have shown how, by the gradual deterioration of their original goodness, men have become what they are' (IV, 935-6).

The form of the work is determined by the principle of chronological development. There are five books of unequal length: the first deals with Emile's early years, stressing the mother's responsibility and the need to avoid undue physical restraints (for example, tight swaddling-clothes which cramp the child's natural movements); the second covers the period from five to twelve years, concentrating on the education of the body and the senses and emphasising the superiority of personal experience over a premature use of bookish methods; the third book deals with Emile's intellectual and vocational education, which will be based on the direct observation of nature and involve the teaching of a manual trade; book four describes moral and religious education from fifteen to twenty and into this book Rousseau inserted a long statement of his own religious beliefs in the form of the *Profession of Faith of the Savoyard Priest*. The fifth, entitled *Sophie ou la Femme, (Sophie or Woman)*, brings the work to a romantic conclusion by providing Emile with his future wife.

In spite of the formal division of his work into five books, Rousseau warns his readers against expecting any rigid and systematic treatment of the subject, for in his preface he speaks of 'this collection of reflections and observations, without order and almost without continuity . . . less a treatise on education than a visionary's reveries on education'. Indeed, many of the characteristics of *Emile* make it more like a novel than a formal treatise, for it is in some ways a kind of imaginary biography interspersed with anecdotes and illustrations drawn from the author's own life, experience and imagination. At the same time, the personal style through which he frequently addresses his readers as a whole, or some particularly important section of them (mothers, fathers, tutors and so on), gives the text a warmth and vividness which support and extend the idealism of its main principles.

It is no accident that one of Rousseau's favourite books — and the only one allowed to young Emile — was *Robinson Crusoe,* for like Defoe's hero, Rousseau starts with the individual in the presence of nature, and in spite of obvious differences, the direct confrontation of the growing individual with the challenge of the physical world remains one of the most striking features of Emile's early life. It is the very absence of artificial social constraints and the reassuring presence of nature herself which explains the freshness and vigour of the book: the child, like Crusoe, has to learn to adapt himself to the 'necessity' of things. As Rousseau makes clear, he is to be brought up in the country far from the fetid atmosphere of cities, and throughout *Emile* it is not simply a question of extolling the merits of the countryside at the expense of the town but of presenting physical nature as the authentic background for the life of a growing child. When at the end of the second book Rousseau pauses to look at his young charge, who is now nearly twelve years old, he is struck by the analogy between his life and the cycle of the seasons, for he sees a close link between the development of the human being and the movement of physical nature. By skilfully appealing to his feelings and imagination as well as to his reason, Rousseau enables the reader to make his own response to the beauty of nature. 'On seeing nature being reborn', he says of the spring, 'one feels oneself being given new life'. He goes on to explain how our imagination adds to the enjoyment of the 'sight of the seasons' since it enriches our vision with the idea of the seasons which are to follow; in the same way we appreciate the happy boy 'given entirely to his immediate being and enjoying the fullness of life which wants to extend itself beyond him', for both Rousseau and the reader cannot help identifying themselves with Emile and at the same time recreating the reality of an experience marked by 'a movement of joy'.

Emile is also close to nature in a somewhat different way in so far as his life and being resemble those of primitive man : like him, he is strong, active and self-sufficient, his reactions being determined by the physical — rather than the human — world. Like the savage too, he is 'without gnawing care, without long and painful forethought, completely given to his present being'. (This last phrase recalls a similar one used to describe primitive man in the second *Discourse)*[2]. Obviously there are important differences between such a boy and the savage, for, in spite of constant efforts to preserve his pupil's 'primitive taste', the educator has to consider the future: if Emile is in some ways a savage dominated by his immediate physical interest, he is also 'a savage intended for the town'. Whereas primitive man remains immured in his immediate condition, Emile is slowly moving towards a higher and more complete stage of existence. It is important, therefore, not to confuse 'what is natural to the savage stage and what is natural to the civil stage', for 'there is a considerable difference between the man living in the state of nature, and natural man living in the state of society' (IV, 483, 764). Nevertheless, in these early years Emile receives his lessons from nature, not from men, and he 'always acts in accordance with his own thoughts and not those of other people.' In spite of his own distinctive character and his future possibilities he is still a 'pupil of nature'.

Throughout his work, Rousseau makes it clear that to live in the presence of nature is to be liberated from the irksome restrictions of society and one of *Emile's* main themes is the importance of freedom — of a freedom that is in striking contrast to the situation of modern man destined for enslavement from the very first days of his existence. At the physical — even physiological — level, freedom means little more than the removal of painful and unnecessary physical constraints and the provision of conditions which do not stifle or distort spontaneous growth. (Hence early education will be largely 'negative'). Though more complex, the child in this respect is not very different from the plant or animal — an analogy which Rousseau had drawn at the very beginning of his work when he urged the mother 'to cultivate and water the young plant before it dies'. Freedom does not mean mere arbitrary licence, but a 'well-organised freedom' which lets the child express the innate needs of his organism and yet makes him face the demands of inescapable 'necessity'. Nature herself will for the most part supply the inevitable limitations imposed upon every finite being, but these will not be an obstacle to its healthy growth.

Since freedom is inseparable from orderly development, the educator has to realize that each stage of human existence has its own kind of 'perfection'. This is particularly true of childhood and it is Rousseau's merit to have made the point — perhaps obvious to the modern world but not to his — that, although the child is destined to become a man, he is not just a man in miniature but has his own unique form of being. Rousseau insists that the educators of his day 'always seek the man in the child without thinking what he is before being a man... Nature wants children to be children before being men. Childhood has ways of seeing, thinking and feeling which are its own; nothing is more foolish than to want to replace them by ours' (IV, 242, 319). That is why he exhorts his readers 'to love childhood and favour its games, pleasures and instinct for life' (IV, 302). The true educator must identify himself with the child and see the world from his point of view. If Rousseau is able to do this, it is, he avers, because of the child-like elements in his own character. 'As I grow older,' he tells his readers, 'I am becoming a child again.' (IV, 385). 'I believe I am living with his life and his vivacity rejuvenates me.' One of the most striking features of *Emile* is the author's constant effort to identify himself with the child's consciousness and to see life and the world from his point of view. In this respect, *Emile* tries to do for the child what the *Discourse on Inequality* had done for primitive man.

It must never be forgotten that a child cannot go beyond the range of his immediate experience; he is essentially a physical, sensuous being whose desires and needs are governed by his appetites and 'present interest'. Since he is concerned only with 'what touches him immediately', it is as useless as it is harmful to burden him with intellectual, moral or religious concepts to which he can attach no meaning. Rousseau takes issue with

Locke on this point : it is futile to reason with a child or to speak to him in abstract language; he must be taught by direct contact with objects. This is why Rousseau insists on bringing up Emile in the countryside, for the constant pressure of nature will show that freedom is compatible with dependence on physical necessity. Words and reasons, on the other hand, are indications that the child is being subjected to 'the arbitrary will of others'. 'It is in man's nature to endure patiently the necessity of things, but not the ill-will of other people' (IV, 320). This is a theme to which Rousseau returns in all his works, for it involves a type of subjection which is, in his opinion, the cause of social injustice and the unhappy enslavement of modern man.

As soon as we remove from the educational process an over-anxious concern for the future and accept childhood as it is, we can treat it as a phase of human existence which, being valuable in its own right, must be made as full and happy as possible. 'As soon as children can feel the pleasure of being, make them enjoy it; at whatever hour God calls them, do not let them die without having tasted life' (IV, 302). A child should not be allowed to lose 'the few moments which nature has given him'; we must let him enjoy the 'fullness of life' which gives reality to the present phase of his existence.

Important though it is in its own right, childhood is but one aspect of human existence. 'Before the vocation of parent, nature calls the individual to human life', so that 'our true study is that of the human condition' (IV 252). In order to obtain a proper understanding of man's true being, it is necessary to cut through the subtlety and refinement of existing prejudices by appealing directly to his essential nature. 'Men, be human, this is your first duty; be so for every condition, every age, for everything that is not alien to man. What wisdom is there for you outside humanity?' 'O man,' he exclaims, 'is it my fault if you have made everything good difficult?' (IV, 325). 'O man, confine your existence within yourself, and you will not be wretched. Remain in the place which nature assigns to you in the chain of beings, and nothing will be able to take you out of it.' The proper understanding of human nature and its indissoluble connections with 'nature' in the larger sense is for Rousseau the incontrovertible basis of all valid experience.

Rousseau's confidence in nature leads him to attach great importance to the principle of 'self-love' (*amour de soi*) as the ultimate constituent of human existence: it is 'the only passion natural to man, the only passion with which he is born and the only one which never leaves him'; it is 'a primitive innate passion preceding any other and of which all the rest are, in a way, only modifications'. As such, it is the source of self-preservation and freedom. Self-love is quite different from the 'pride' (*amour-propre*) which originates in society and replaces the 'gentle affectionate passions born from self-love' by 'hateful irascible passions' derived from social man's constant comparison of himself with other people and his permanent struggle for mastery and domination. Because self-love is natural, it is quite compatible with the principle of order and the expansive feelings which give rise to 'goodness, humanity and benevolence'. Already in his primitive state man could experience 'natural pity' and this sentiment was subsequently developed by memory and imagination, so that he could achieve personal happiness and yet extend his feelings beyond himself.

Since this expansive movement originates in the heart, reason has to accept a subordinate place in the hierarchy of human powers and, although it is not inactive at an early stage, it cannot be separated from the effects of *sensibilité*. Mistaken views of reason are probably due, thinks Rousseau, to the false assumption that it is a single autonomous faculty, whereas 'it is a compound of all the rest and one that develops last and with the greatest difficulty' (IV, 317). The chief limitation of reason is that it cannot rely on itself or provide an adequate inspiration to human endeavour. A child, according to Rousseau, has images, not ideas, for his experience results from contact with physical objects; ideas, on the other hand, presuppose an understanding of complex relationships. Whereas imagining involves seeing and is thus bound up with the passive experience of sensations, intellectual perception requires the cooperation of an active judgement. Nevertheless, the child's limited understanding does not prevent him from making some use of his reason, but this has to be related to his immediate physical interests. Children do not reason about the future, affirms Rousseau, but about their present desires. The early development of their reason, therefore, helps to bring them into a more meaningful relationship with the external world. This is the function of what Rousseau calls 'sensitive reason' (*la raison sensible*) as opposed to the 'intellectual reason' (*la raison intellectuelle*) used in maturity. 'Our first masters of philosophy are our feet, hand and eyes' (IV, 370). That is why in the early stages of human intelligence our limbs and organs are regarded as its 'instruments'. In short, 'far from man's true reason being formed independently of his body, it is the body's good constitution which makes the mind's operations easy and sure'. Rousseau praises enlightened predecessors like Montaigne and Locke for having stressed the importance of physical education in childhood.

While not denying the value of reason, Rousseau insists that its effective functioning requires the support of other aspects of the personality; it cannot rely on itself. 'Reason alone is not active: it sometimes restrains, it rarely arouses and it has never done anything great. To be for ever reasoning is the obsession of small minds. Great souls have another language' (IV, 645). This is made very clear in the fourth book of *Emile* which analyses the emergence of moral values and concepts. Rousseau seeks to show how these emerge from the orderly and progressive development of human powers and especially from the 'feelings and knowledge relative to our constitution'. Words like 'justice' and 'reason' do not indicate merely abstract notions but 'true affections of the soul enlightened by reason', for they are 'only the orderly progress of our primitive affections'. 'By reason alone, independently of conscience, one can establish no natural law; and every natural right is only a chimera if it is not based on a natural need of the human heart' (IV, 523).

With the appearance of morality Rousseau's philosophy moves in two directions: in the first place, morality is inseparable from a man's relations with his fellow-men (already in the preface to his play *Narcisse* Rousseau had insisted that 'vice' and 'virtue' were social concepts) and so leads ultimately to politics. The passage from *Emile* just quoted is followed by the statement that 'those who want to treat morality and politics separately will never understand anything of either' (IV, 525). Secondly, morality involves a deepening of the inner life, and this leads to the emergence of conscience as the fundamental impulse behind ethical decisions. Though profoundly personal, conscience is not capricious and subjective, for Rousseau sees it as the divine element in human existence; in a well-known passage in the *Profession of Faith* he hails it as the 'inner voice' which never deceives us: the 'divine instinct, immortal and celestial voice, the certain guide of a being ignorant and limited, but intelligent and free; infallible judge of good and evil, you who make man like God, it is you who form the excellence of his nature and the morality of his actions. Without you I feel nothing in me which lifts me above the beasts' (IV, 600-1). Conscience is expressed through principles 'written in the depth of our heart in indelible characters'. 'So there is in the depth of our souls an innate principle of justice and virtue on which, in spite of our own maxims, [i.e. those derived from our life in corrupt society] we judge our actions and those of other people as good or bad, and it is to this principle that I give the name of conscience' (IV, 598). However weak or hesitant it may be in contemporary society, it is a principle of universal validity and belongs to man's original being. As soon as the individual withdraws into himself and escapes from the corrupting influence of his environment, he can listen to this inner voice and understand its true meaning.

Although conscience may often appear strange to men unaccustomed to acknowledging their own true nature, it is not a divisive element in the human personality. On the contrary, its messages can often be clarified by the use of reason and expressed by the activity of the will. 'Has not God given me conscience to love the good, reason to know it and freedom to choose it?' (IV, 605). Only thus can man attain the 'supreme felicity' which should be the goal of his existence.

If conscience has a universal aspect, it is largely because of its divine origins, and this, in turn, means that it is related to the principle of order which, according to Rousseau, lies at the very centre of God's creation. Contrary to a widespread belief that it is simply the result of social 'prejudice', conscience 'persists in following the order of nature against all the laws of men' (IV, 566). Indeed, human wisdom consists of using freedom as a means of following 'the general order'. As the

Savoyard priest insists, 'I see in the system of the world an order which does not belie itself' (IV, 588).

It is in the *Profession of Faith of the Savoyard Priest* inserted in the fourth book of *Emile* that Rousseau has given the most extended and systematic account of his religious beliefs. (A later and briefer statement is to be found in the letter he sent in 1769 to a young man called Franquières). If the discussion of religion is deferred to a comparatively late stage in Emile's education, it is largely because, in Rousseau's opinion, the slow development of reason does not allow a boy to have any clear ideas of religious truth before the age of fourteen. The religious issue, however, will be discussed here in connection with Rousseau's philosophy of man rather than in any specifically pedagogic context. The fierce hostility which followed the publication of the *Profession of Faith* is to be explained — as far as orthodox Christians, and especially Roman Catholics, were concerned — by Rousseau's stress upon natural religion as something that every sincere man can discover for himself by the 'good use of his faculties', that is, by consulting the two sources already indicated in the analysis of morality — the inner self and the external world. 'Has not God', asks Rousseau, 'said everything to our eyes, conscience and judgement? What else will men say to us?' 'Look at the sight of nature,' he concludes, 'listen to the inner voice' (IV, 607).

As soon as he can use his understanding, man should be able, insists Rousseau, to establish his place in the universe, for the harmony and order experienced within his own being will be reflected in the harmony and order of physical nature. In each case, however, it is a question of the spiritual reality mirrored in the physical order instead of the material world being considered for its own sake. When Rousseau sets out to examine the question of God's existence in the first part of the *Profession*, he uses a form of argument which is apt to give a misleading impression of his religious beliefs. This long and not very convincing metaphysical analysis of the proofs of God's existence was a late addition to the text and was prompted by his growing anxiety about the rapid spread of philosophical materialism; he was worried especially by the influence of Helvétius, whose *De L'Esprit* had been published in 1758. Rousseau wanted to show that even at the abstract intellectual level materialism could be effectively refuted, although he himself relied but little on this kind of 'proof'. In any case, he did not deny that reason ought to play a vital role in any discussion of religious belief which involved the rational as well as the affective aspects of man's being, and in the second part of the *Profession* he went so far as to affirm that 'all ideas about the Divinity come from reason alone'.

In this respect, his arguments owe something to the deism which had been widely accepted in the first half of the eighteenth century; he indicates his admiration for the great apologist of deism, Samuel Clarke, the English divine, whose *Being and Attributes of God* had given him a European reputation. Rousseau describes Clarke as a thinker capable of 'illuminating the world, finally heralding the Being of beings and Dispenser of things'. 'What universal admiration, what unanimous applause would have greeted this new system, so great, so consoling, so sublime, so suitable for uplifting the soul, providing a basis for virtue, and at the same time, so striking, luminous and simple; it seems to offer fewer incomprehensible things to the human mind than the absurdities it finds in any other system' (IV, 570). The eulogy of Clarke is repeated in the letter to Franquières when Rousseau links his name with Plato's (IV, 1135).[3]

Clarke was only one of the English thinkers who had contributed to the spread of French deism, for such works as Locke's *Reasonableness of Christianity* (1695) and Toland's *Christianity not Mysterious* (1696) were followed by the writings of Collins, Tindal, Woolston and Bolingbroke, who were becoming known in France. French deism, however, did not have to rely on foreign sources, for Descartes had already tried to establish rational proofs for the existence of God and at the same time to present a view of matter which led to a mechanistic view of the world as a material substance governed by the laws of cause and effect; if God created this world, he did not intervene directly since it could function effectively in accordance with its own mechanism.

In spite of the basic differences between Descartes's metaphysical and Newton's scientific outlook, both considered the universe to be governed by the laws of physics and mathematics and ultimately accepted the same mechanistic model. Admittedly, Newton had affirmed that God could intervene from time to time to readjust any faults in the functioning of the physical world, but this was a point to which his French followers paid little heed. It seemed to many thinkers, however, that both Descartes and Newton could be treated as supporters of deism. Voltaire, for example, explicitly based his own deistic views on Newton's work. In such cases God was not a personal presence, but a somewhat remote Being who, after creating the Universe, let it function according to its own laws.

In spite of its deistic implications, this mechanistic view of the universe also led some thinkers away from religion towards philosophical materialism, as they began to see physical reality as a self-regulating process which had no need of a divine creator. Moreover, the mechanistic explanation was readily extended to the human mind which, being assimilated to other forms of matter, was held to depend on the functioning of bodily organs. It was the apparently rapid spread of this mechanistic materialism which, as we have seen, induced Rousseau to attack the materialists with their own intellectual weapons.

The metaphysical section of the *Profession of Faith* seems to accept a mechanistic view of matter that was common to both deists and materialists in so far as it stresses the idea of the inertia of matter; matter is a passive substance which, being incapable of generating its own movement, requires a divine creator; on the other hand, Rousseau takes over the Cartesian idea of the mind as a uniquely active immaterial substance and, on the analogy of the human will as a power that can initiate action, argues that God as Creator must be both supreme intelligence and supreme will. At the same time the unique activity of mind and judgement guarantees the immateriality — and finally the immortality — of the soul. The kind of materialism which Rousseau tries so hard to refute must already have seemed somewhat out-of-date to thinkers who were paying greater attention to the new developments in biology and the 'sciences of life' than to the future of mathematical physics. Such was certainly the case with Diderot, who rejected mechanistic materialism in favour of a more dynamic form based on the principle of sensitivity. The revival of interest in such ancient thinkers as Lucretius and Epicurus, as well as the persistence of Leibniz's view of the monad as a centre of force and energy, lent support to a form of materialism that seemed to be more consistent with the findings of modern science than the old-fashioned materialism. That the enthusiastic welcome given to 'spontaneous generation' eventually proved premature did not deter bolder minds from seeing the universe as a vast animal or living organism, rather than as a lifeless though infinitely complex mechanism.

That Rousseau would not have been inclined to participate in this kind of philosophical debate, had it not been for the publication of new materialistic works, is revealed by the late insertion of the metaphysical argument into the manuscript.[4] Moreover, his own personal preference had always been for a different approach to the philosophical interpretation of the external world. He makes it clear in the *Confessions* that he was drawn to works which combined science and religion in a closer and more purposeful way than the Cartesian-style deism. As well as Bernard Lamy's *Entretiens sur les Sciences* to which reference has already been made, Rousseau probably knew the abbé Pluche's *The Sight of Nature or Conversations on Natural History and the Sciences* (*Le Spectacle de la Nature ou Entretiens sur l'histoire naturelle et les sciences*), (1732-49), a work that was extremely popular in the eighteenth century and was translated into several European languages. Voltaire praised it as 'an estimable work'. Pluche sought to demonstrate God's presence in his creation as a kind of 'primitive revelation': order and creativity were especially apparent in plants and animals, since each species was considered to have been formed in accordance with a specific plan, the unity of the whole design corresponding to that of the intelligence responsible for it. Many thinkers were no longer content to view the universe in mathematical and mechanistic terms. Lord Shaftesbury, for example, whose *Essay on Virtue and Merit* (1709) had been translated and annotated by Diderot, was praised by Rousseau who spoke of 'the virtuous Shaftesbury and his worthy interpreter': apart from stressing the importance of an innate moral sense, Shaftesbury advocated a form of theism which affirmed the goodness of God's creation and man's ability to respond to it through his senses and emotions as well as through his reason. Pope's optimism, to which Rousseau also subscribed, probably owed something to Shaftesbury's influence. Support for a purposive view of the physical world was also forthcoming from various scientists: the Dutch doctor Bernard Nieuwentyt (1654-1718) defended final causes in a much-read work, *The Religious Philosopher and the Right Use of Contemplating the Works of the Creator* (1718), while Réaumur (1683-1757), a many-sided scientist who was mathematician, physicist and naturalist, in a remarkable work, *Mémoires pour servir à l'Histoire des Insectes* (1734-42), described the marvels of the insect-world. Moreover, these particular contributions to the analysis of God's creation remained indebted to a metaphysical tradition that was still mindful of Plato and had, to a large extent, been renewed by Descartes, Leibniz and Spinoza; particularly relevant to the present topic was the work of Malebranche, whose *Entretiens métaphysiques* had stressed the principle of order and its relationship to God's goodness, an idea to which Rousseau, as we have seen, was always very sympathetic.

In the course of the eighteenth century, the metaphysical framework used for the interpretation of God and nature became associated with a view that laid greater stress on feeling and sensibility than on reason. The impersonal mechanistic view associated with Descartes and Newton no longer satisfied those who, like Rousseau, were seeking a closer link between God's creation and the resources of man's inner life. In any case, whatever may have been the precise philosophical sources of Rousseau's religious outlook, he himself was never prepared to rely solely on abstract argument to prove the existence of spiritual truths. Although the rapid advance of contemporary materialism led him to undertake its philosophical refutation, his own acceptance of the principle of universal 'order' did not in the first place depend on intellectual proof. Although he believed that the rational justification of religion was desirable and necessary when it was made the subject of intellectual debate, his own approach to the physical world elicited a more intense and convincing kind of response than one that could be provided by the mind alone. Man, he believed, is not impelled towards God by some purely mental need, but by the prompting of his inner being; he feels a desire to identify himself with a universal order that satisfies his heart and conscience as well as his mind; the spiritual and affective aspects of the human personality provide an intense and often overwhelming motive for accepting God's existence. This is made quite explicit in his last work, *The Reveries of the Lonely Walker.* 'The rural solitude in which I spent the best years of my youth, the study of good books to which I wholeheartedly devoted myself, strengthened my natural tendency to affectionate feelings and made me devout almost like Fénelon. Meditation in seclusion, the study of nature, the contemplation of the universe impel a lonely man to move constantly towards the author of all things and to seek with a gentle concern the end of all he sees and the cause of all he feels' (I, 1013-4).

Because man is drawn to God by various motives, all the principal elements in his personality will be brought into play. The numerous 'quibbles' and 'metaphysical subtleties' put forward by the opponents of religion will not carry any weight when they are set against 'fundamental principles adopted by my reason, confirmed by my heart and stamped with the seal of inner assent when the passions are still'. One difficult intellectual objection will not overthrow 'a whole body of doctrine, so solid, so coherent and fashioned with so much meditation and care and so well suited to my reason, my heart and my whole being, and strengthened by the inner assent which I feel to be lacking in all the rest' (I, 1018).

Apart from the combined effect of these personal motives, Rousseau is convinced that there is a close connection between the structure of man's being and that of the external world: no merely intellectual objections can ever destroy the 'congruity which I feel to exist between my immortal nature and the constitution of this world and the physical order which I see prevailing in it. In the corresponding moral order and the system resulting from my researches, I find the support I need to bear the miseries of this life. In any other system I should die without any resources and without hope. I should be the most wretched of creatures' (I, 1018-9). Religion, therefore, is inwardly consoling and at the same time rooted in a reality that is greater than human existence, since it forms part of the universal order governing all things.

An appeal to the consoling aspects of his religious system had already been characteristic of Rousseau's earlier attitude. Although the long letter written to Voltaire in 1756 on the subject of Providence (Rousseau had been anxious to refute the pessimism of Voltaire's *Poem on the Lisbon Earthquake* of 1755) had contained an extended metaphysical argument based on the optimism of Leibniz and Pope, this had been preceded and followed by an almost aggressive affirmation of personal feelings. 'Pope's poem alleviates my ills and makes me patient; yours aggravates my troubles, arouses my protests and, taking everything from me except a tottering hope, reduces me to despair.' At the end of his letter Rousseau reminds his correspondent of the great difference between their personal situations and attitudes; whereas the rich and successful Voltaire, living in the midst of fame and luxury, finds only evil on earth, the 'obscure, poor and lonely man, tormented by an incurable illness' believes that 'all is for the best'. The source of this contradiction is clear. 'You enjoy, but I hope, and hope beautifies everything'. However brilliant and imposing Voltaire's arguments may be, 'all the subtleties of metaphysics will never make me doubt for one moment the immortality of the soul and the beneficence of Providence. I feel it, I believe, I wish it, I hope for it, I shall defend it to my last breath' (IV, 1059-75).

Although it is possible to find a metaphysical — almost Platonic — element in Rousseau's religious thought since everything finally depends on the notion of universal order, the merely philosophical aspect is less important than the appeal to human sensitivity, and it is undoubtedly this which exerted the greatest influence on Rousseau's contemporaries and successors. The *Profession of Faith* was part of a wide movement which gradually led to the religious revival signalled first by Chateaubriand's work of Christian apologetics, *The Genius of Christianity* (1802), and then by the Romantics' support of religious values. The ultimate appeal of Rousseau's religious writings, in spite of his own insistence that they could be justified on rational grounds, depended more on their emotional and aesthetic attractions than on their philosophical content. Apart from his use of sources of inspiration largely ignored by the leading thinkers of the Enlightenment, Rousseau's religious outlook re-established the close link between man's inner life and the spiritual essence of the physical universe; to perceive and appreciate this link, man had to rely on his soul rather than on his mind alone. Moreover, the posthumous publication of Rousseau's auto-biographical writings — the *Letters to Malesherbes*, the *Confessions* and the *Reveries of the Lonely Walker* — lent powerful support to this newly discovered religious feeling for nature since they contained a vivid and often intense lyrical account of his spiritual response to the physical world.

The introduction of the religious issue into the fourth book of *Emile* sets the work within a broader philosophical context and provides the metaphysical principles by which human existence can be properly understood. Yet this cannot be the complete answer to the problem of man's destiny on earth. Although God and nature form the ultimate basis of any adequate philosophy of man, the developing individual is still faced with the task of establishing relations with other people. Emile's early education was determined primarily by contact with things — rather than with people — and he was confronted by the 'necessity' of the physical world rather than by the 'arbitrary will of men'. He was able, therefore, to express the innate possibilities of his being in a way that brought him all the fulfilment and 'perfection' of which he was capable. As Rousseau constantly affirms, Emile is a being who experiences genuine joy in living. As he grows older, however, he is made to realize that 'necessity' is not confined to the physical world and that preparation for life involves obligations to others as well as the experience of one's own happiness. The emergence of sexual desire also means that one day Emile will undertake the responsibilities of marriage and family life. This, in turn, leads to his eventual participation in society.

The fifth book of *Emile*, entitled *Sophie or Woman*, is far less original than the rest. Whereas the earlier parts had put forward radical views which challenged the assumptions of contemporary practice, the ideas about women's education are extremely conservative, even reactionary. Women exist, it would seem, to serve and obey men — to be wives, mothers and housekeepers — and their education should be directed to this end. Rousseau does not suggest that they are inferior to men but simply that they are different: 'such is the law of nature'. He insists, however, that if husbands rule over the 'person' of their wives, the latter rule over the 'heart' of their husbands, so that as well as exhorting the wife 'to honour her chief', Rousseau tells the husband 'to love his companion'. Women thus play a vital role in society, for they provide the indispensable moral order without which it could not survive. As Rousseau had forcefully put it in the *Letter to d'Alembert*, 'never has a people perished through excess of wine, all perish through the disorder of women' (p. 147).

If the last book of *Emile* is different from the rest, it is not only because it presents a very conservative view of women, but also because it is more like a novel than a treatise, Rousseau no doubt tending to see the relationship between Emile and Sophie in terms of his own romantic fantasies. More significant than this, however, is the curious amalgamation of idealistic feelings and moral values which becomes increasingly apparent as the work draws to its close.

In this fifth book Rousseau takes the opportunity to re-affirm the point so frequently made throughout — that life is meant to be enjoyed. The only thing that Emile must be in a hurry to do is 'to enjoy life'. 'Shall I add, to do good when he can? No, for that too is enjoying life' (IV, 771). 'I have not brought up my Emile to desire or to wait, but to enjoy ... For him to live and to enjoy are the same thing'. It follows from this that he will be constantly savouring the reality of his immediate existence rather than pursuing some distant goal. 'Let us make him happy at every age lest, after so many cares, he dies before he has been happy.' It is a completely 'false prudence' which 'sacrifices the present to the future'.

The enjoyment which should characterise a boy's life is merely the expression of every human being's fundamental need. 'It is necessary to be happy, dear Emile: that is the aim of every sensitive being; that is the last desire imprinted upon us by nature, and the only one which never leaves us.' Yet true happiness, as Rousseau is careful to point out, involves far more than immediate pleasure. Although the child's life has its own distinctive qualities and its own type of perfection, it represents only one stage on 'nature's road'; the perfection of a particular moment cannot be completely separated from the one that follows. Life is aspiration as well as enjoyment and the boy is gradually led to look 'beyond himself'. Within him there is an excess of energy which impels him 'to cast into the future so to speak the surplus of his present being'. At first the individual's weakness makes him concentrate his energies within himself, but as soon as he attains a condition of 'power and strength', the desire to extend his being 'carries him beyond himself and makes him move forward as far as possible' (IV, 427, 430).

As he goes from one phase of existence to the next, man is aware of a change in the very quality of his experience. As long as he was close to 'nature' in its simplest and most innocent forms, he could rely on the power of his 'innate goodness' — 'this absolute goodness which makes a thing what it ought to be by its nature'.[5] Yet this presupposes an ability to remain satisfied with immediate experience. Now, although man's ultimate goal is 'the supreme enjoyment which is contentment with oneself', he has to recognize that the spontaneous impulses of his inner being are not enough to sustain him in all the difficulties of life. 'He who is merely good remains so only so long as he finds pleasure in being good: goodness breaks and perishes at the shock of human passions; the man who is merely good is good only for himself' (IV, 818).

This does not mean that the passions are bad in themselves, but that they may be diverted from their true function by the artificial pressures and constraints of social life. It is wrong to classify the passions into 'good and 'bad'. 'All are good when you remain master of them. All are bad when you let yourself be subjugated by them . . . It does not depend on us to have or not to have passions; but it depends on us to rule over them . . . Any feeling which a man dominates is legitimate, any which dominates him is criminal' (IV, 819). To the impetus of natural goodness must be added the strengthening power of the will, so that man can become virtuous as well as good. 'There is no happiness without courage, or virtue without a struggle. The word "virtue" comes from "strength" and strength is the basis of all virtue. Virtue belongs to a being weak by nature, but strong by will, and it is that alone which constitutes the merit of the just man' (IV, 817). Hitherto Emile has been confronted by nothing but external necessity; he must now learn how to resist certain impulses in his own nature whenever they are likely to conflict with his obligations towards other people. It is, therefore, not enough to follow feeling, because virtue demands the cooperation of both reason and conscience. 'What is the virtuous man? It is one who can conquer his affections; for he then follows his reason and his conscience; he does his duty; he obeys the principle of order and nothing can divert him from it.' In short, the virtuous man secures a firmer basis for his existence than the satisfaction of transitory desires, for he is attached to 'the beauty which does not perish and extends the law of necessity to moral matters'. This moral force gives his existence a firmness and continuity that protect him against the uncertainty of fortune and the turbulence of passion.

Rousseau is careful to insist that the attainment of virtue is a perfectly natural goal for the fully developed individual. Liberated from the constricting effects of narrow self-interest, he can abandon himself to 'transports of admiration for heroic actions and raptures of love for great souls'. Enthusiasm for virtue, like the love of beauty from which it is inseparable, leads to a form of personal fulfilment which is quite consistent with the 'supreme enjoyment' and 'the pure pleasure springing from contentment with oneself'. Far from leaving the individual inwardly divided, morality gives him a higher sense of personal unity, for he has used 'his conscience to love the good, reason to know it and freedom to choose it'.

Above all else, morality, insists Rousseau, leads to a new understanding of freedom. It is no longer a question of the 'natural freedom' of the primitive man who relied solely on his own strength to satisfy his desires; it is also far more than the limited freedom of the young child who was aware of little more than physical needs. Throughout *Emile* Rousseau has related the expression of freedom to the requirement of 'order' and already in the second book he calls attention to the importance of 'well-regulated freedom' as a cardinal principle. In the early years the educator's function has been largely negative, because he has sought to remove the artificial barriers which prevent the child from facing the inescapable necessity of the physical world. As soon as freedom is transformed into an internal principle, it acquires a more positive meaning, for the mature man is his own master inasmuch as he has learned to control his inner life in accordance with moral demands. He realizes that freedom is henceforth to be identified with will: 'the principle of all action is in the will of a free being' and 'there is no true will without freedom'. There thus appears to be a Stoic element in Rousseau's moral outlook, for feelings are now subjected to a firm inner law.

The presence of this Stoic aspect does not eliminate the importance of happiness and enjoyment. Nature remains the guiding principle of human behaviour, even though it has now been given a moral dimension. The wise man learns how to adjust desire to capacity. 'The truly free man wants only what he can obtain and he does what pleases him' (IV, 309). He is content to 'remain in his place,' recognizing that freedom and power ought not to go beyond his 'natural strength'. 'O man, remain in the place which nature assigns to you in the chain of beings and nothing will be able to remove you from it.'

Freedom still retains a genuinely personal quality, for it involves the fulfilment of a man's inner being, but this fulfilment, being related to the principle of order, also makes him look beyond himself towards his relations with other people; it is not until he relates his own needs to the life of others that his existence can become truly moral. After directing his energies upon his 'physical relations with other beings', Emile is finally led to acknowledge his 'moral relations with other men'. Indeed, genuine moral values cannot emerge without the establishment of some form of social life. As Rousseau insisted in an early work (the introduction to his play *Narcisse*), 'these words "virtues and vices" are collective notions which originate only in human intercourse' (II, 97n.).

Yet human relations cannot remain merely general and abstract, which is perhaps another reason why the fifth book of *Emile* is in many ways like a novel. Emile is being prepared not only for marriage but also for a way of life that may require him to sacrifice personal interest to the common good. Although he seems to have found bliss with Sophie — 'the man who can prolong the happiness of love into marriage will have found paradise on earth' (IV, 608) — the family is intended to form part of a larger community. Rousseau, therefore, ends his work with a description of the society to which Emile will belong. Needless to say, this is not to be found near 'great cities'. 'One of the examples which good people can give to the rest is that of a patriarchal life, the first life of man, the most peaceful, the most natural and the most agreeable to the uncorrupted heart.' There follows an idyllic picture of the life which Emile and Sophie will be able to lead in such an environment. 'I am moved as I think how many benefits Emile and Sophie, from their simple retreat, can spread around them, how they can enliven the countryside and revive the zeal of the unfortunate villagers. I imagine the population increasing, the fields growing fertile, the earth taking on a new adornment, plenty and abundance transforming labours into holidays, joyful cries and blessings arising from the midst of the rural games around the young couple who have revived them. People call the golden age a daydream and it will always be one for anybody with a corrupt heart and taste. It is not even true that people regret the golden age, since these regrets are always futile. What then would be required to restore it? One thing, and an impossible one — to love it.'

In his description of the rural community centred on Emile and Sophie, Rousseau is to some extent following his emotions and imagination as well as his reason and, in one of his favourite expressions, he is portraying 'a society after his own heart'. That such a life is exposed to constant threat from the outside world is clearly shown by Rousseau's intention of providing a sequel to *Emile — Emile et Sophie ou Les Solitaires*. Emile and Sophie were to be taken from their idyllic environment and exposed to various hazards, Sophie herself falling from virtue, only to be redeemed in the end by Emile's loyalty and devotion.

Already in *Emile* itself Rousseau had indicated that moral freedom cannot be limited to a social life that does not make severe demands upon the individual. Moreover, the happiness of an idyllic rural life is vouchsafed to only very few people. The conditions of real life are such that men have to belong to some form of political society and each individual has to be a 'citizen' as well as a 'man'. It is significant, therefore, that

Rousseau should have included a summary of the *Social Contract* in the fifth book of *Emile*. Although Emile had been prepared for society in a broadly human way, he had not been compelled to adapt himself to political institutions. It remained for Rousseau to explain the principles which would inspire a political society composed of men who, like Emile, had come to a full awareness of their own true nature. It was not accidental that *Emile* should have been published in the same year as the *Social Contract*.

4. Emotion and Morality

Before the appearance of *Emile* and the *Social Contract*, Rousseau had made a sustained imaginative effort to describe an ideal society through the composition of his novel *Julie ou la Nouvelle Héloïse*, which was published in 1761. This work is not usually considered to be a major source of Rousseau's ideas, for, as a novel, it lends itself more readily to literary than to philosophical analysis, but the presence of a strongly didactic element, especially in the latter parts, has led at least one critic to find in it a 'synthesis of Rousseau's thought'.[1] Even a cursory reading of the book reveals an obvious link between its view of society and the conception of communal life briefly described at the end of *Emile*. Moreover, the tensions and ambiguities of the novel, which are connected with Rousseau's attempt to reconcile the needs of emotion, imagination and reflection by transforming an erotic fantasy into a moral treatise, cannot be ignored in any serious attempt to present a comprehensive account of his philosophy.

In the *Confessions* he has written at some length about the origins of his novel. In 1756 the generosity of a wealthy friend, Mme d'Epinay, who offered him the use of a rural property called 'The Hermitage', enabled him to move from Paris to the forest of Montmorency. Hoping henceforth to escape from the irksome aspects of his Parisian environment, he proposed to continue his life and work in conditions suited to his needs and character. To achieve this end he carried out a number of moral and physical 'reforms' aimed at simplifying his material existence and improving the quality of his inner life. At first he tried to realise this rural idyll with the help of his companion Thérèse Levasseur; although she was ignorant and illiterate, he insists that she was a 'person after his own heart' and one who could 'share his most tender affections'. Unfortunately, however, this did not allow him to overcome the difficulties of his situation: apart from the limitations of Thérèse herself, her greedy and scheming mother, who also came to live with them, was constantly upsetting him by pestering his friends for money or by involving other members of her family in her intrigues.

These frustrations, together with the nagging memory of the illegitimate children whom he had abandoned to the Found-lings' Home, exposed him to a disturbing inner contradiction. On the one hand, there was his overwhelming need for 'plenitude' and complete enjoyment, and, on the other hand, an inescapable feeling of 'emptiness'. Indeed the terms 'full' ('fullness') and 'empty' ('emptiness') are constantly alternating in his account of this period of his life. In particular, he was aware that his 'expansive soul' was 'devoured' by the need to love and be loved, while his 'combustible senses' merely strengthened his longing for an ideal companion. His unful-filled need for love thus let him be consumed by a 'devouring but barren flame'.

The psychological consequences of this state of mind were serious, for they made Rousseau turn away from immediate reality and retreat into his own being. To alleviate his frustration he began to imagine himself as a young man who had fallen in love with a girl created from the idealised memories of the various women he had known in his youth. Surrounded by a 'seraglio of Houris', he was suddenly transformed from the 'serious citizen of Geneva' concerned with moral values into an 'extravagant shepherd' leading a life of 'seductive softness' (I, 427). He found such pleasure in 'hovering in the Empyrean amid the charming objects by which he was surrounded' that he spent whole days in this 'enchanted world' and in the 'society of perfect beings' capable of satisfying his overwhelming need for love and friendship. He imagined he had two female friends with 'analogous but different characters, one dark, the other fair, one lively, the other gentle, the one sensible, the other weak'. 'I gave to one of them a lover of whom the other was a tender friend and even something more', but there was no rivalry or enmity between them because he could never let his imagination dwell on any 'painful feeling'. 'Enamoured by my two charming models, I identified myself with the lover and friend as much as possible; but I made him lovable and young, endowing him besides with the virtues and defects which I felt were mine' (I, 430). After some hesitation he gave to his fantasies a setting remembered from his past — the lake of Geneva to which he had always been so strongly attached. At first, he merely wrote a 'few scattered and disconnected letters', but the writer soon began to take control of the dreamer and a vague plan eventually assumed the definite form of a novel.

During this time further complications were being brought to Rousseau's existence, first by his quarrel with Diderot, whose friendship he publicly repudiated in a comment added to the *Letter to d'Alembert*, and then by his passion for Mme d'Epinay's sister-in-law, the young and vivacious Mme d'Houdetot, mistress of the soldier-poet the Marquis de Saint-Lambert. Although Rousseau had planned the novel and written a good deal of it before his encounter with Mme d'Houdetot, this incident undoubtedly had some influence on its final form. At first Rousseau claimed that he did not intend to publish the work, but he eventually changed his mind and it appeared in January 1761, having already been published in London at the end of the previous year.

As its personal origins will have made clear, *La Nouvelle Héloïse* is very different from Rousseau's other writings. A novel of passion was an unexpected production from an author who had so severely condemned the uncontrolled emotionalism of the theatre and the moral decadence of modern culture. For some time, however, Rousseau seems to have hesitated about the novel's exact form, apparently intending it first of all to consist of four parts and subsequently extending it to six in order to give fuller expression to his growing concern with moral and religious issues. *La Nouvelle Héloïse* finally emerges as a hybrid work, a curious compound of formal literature, personal fantasy and moral and religious didacticism; as such, it is not entirely satisfactory as novel, confession or moral treatise. Nevertheless, it is undoubtedly one of Rousseau's most characteristic and revealing works, for he put into it many intimate emotions and aspirations, often unwittingly confessing himself in a less self-conscious way than in the personal writings, and abandoning himself to his imagination in the portrayal of characters who, without being the direct embodiment of his own divided self, expressed his most secret longings. At the same time he was able to indulge in some of his favourite dreams, describing in idyllic terms the happy life of the countryside (as opposed to the wretched corruption of city life) and the attractions of a small intimate community. Into this novel Rousseau also introduced a multitude of reflections on all kinds of subjects ranging from such specific moral issues as suicide and marital fidelity to more general ideas about education and religion.

These complex motives produced a work which hovered uncertainly between idealism and reality. However great may have been the force of Rousseau's imagination, he could never abandon himself to mere fantasies, for he had to retain some links with the real world and the demands of his own being. Moreover, since his intimate feelings were often ambiguous and contradictory, he finally sought to resolve the ensuing conflict by moving on to a higher moral and spiritual level. Since Jean-Jacques the erotic dreamer had to be reconciled with Rousseau the moral teacher, it was necessary for him to discover a mode of experience, however imaginative its expression, which would unite these two aspects of his being.

The first part of the novel is dominated by intense passion: Julie and her young tutor Saint-Preux fall in love with each other and exchange letters which glow with the idealistic fervour of true love. At first sight it would seem that the two young people are perfectly matched: they have 'uniform ways of feeling and seeing' and 'a certain unison of souls which is immediately perceived' (II, 125). 'Heaven has made us for each other', declares Julie. 'Never was there such a perfect union: our souls, too closely intermingled, can no longer be separated' (II, 212). Their love is unique and 'outside the common rule'. In short, these 'beautiful souls' seem to express the 'sacred law of nature'; they burn with the 'divine fire' of a 'pure and ardent love' which imbues instincts with an 'image of perfection'. Such love almost transcends the limitations of everyday life and leads to the 'supreme felicity' of 'paradise on earth' (II, 51).

Unfortunately, Julie's father, Baron d'Etange, obsessed with his social status, will not let her marry a commoner and contemptuously rejects Saint-Preux as a possible suitor; by so doing, he seems to be profaning 'eternal love' with the vulgarity and insensitivity of a social prejudice that ignores the 'true voice of nature'. As Saint-Preux puts it, 'before your father's tyranny, nature had united us to each other'. As Julie also says, 'we were made for each other and I should be his if the human order had not disturbed the relations of nature' (II, 340). This situation is thus typical of Rousseau's famous dichotomy between 'nature' and 'society', which is now given lyrical and almost poetic intensity. It was undoubtedly this mood of heart-felt idealism which explains the enthusiasm of many contemporary readers for a novel that seemed to open up a whole new world of emotional experience.

Fearing her father's opposition, Julie sends Saint-Preux away for a short time into the mountains of Valais. The young man establishes himself at Meillerie on the other side of the lake. At first the mountain air and scenery bring him a feeling of inner peace: high above the dwellings of other men, he is filled with a sense of purity and sublimity. The sight of 'a new world' and 'another nature' serves to sharpen his mind and his senses to the point of making him forget his own individual identity as he loses himself in the almost supernatural magic of his surroundings. Nevertheless, his continued separation from Julie eventually plunges him into a mood of deep melancholy which 'makes him find everywhere in objects the same horror as prevails within himself: the whole of nature is dead to my eyes as hope is dead in the depth of my heart' (II,90). Seeing in the wildness of the mountain scenery a reflection of his own tormented feelings, Saint-Preux believes that without Julie the world is empty. This consciousness of a close emotional affinity between the inner self and the physical world was to become a commonplace of Romanticism, but Rousseau's novel is one of its earliest and most eloquent examples.

Made desperate by her father's opposition, Julie decides, soon after Saint-Preux's return, to give herself to him. The experience makes him feel that 'one night, one single night has changed his entire soul for ever' (II, 337). Henceforth he will be haunted by an unforgettable memory. 'I am no longer anything', he constantly affirms, 'a single moment has taken everything from me' (II, 191). Since it is Julie who gives him being and substance, — 'But I, Julie alas! a wanderer, without family and almost without fatherland, I have only you on earth and love alone takes the place of everything' (II, 73) — he feels that his love has absolute value and that the physical possession of Julie is but a means of achieving his aim of complete personal fulfilment. Yet because he depends so completely on her and 'exists only through her', he is 'no longer anything for himself and his whole being is related only to her' (II, 56).

Although Saint-Preux's passion is apparently absolute and complete, aspiring, as he puts it, to the attainment of an 'infinite good', it is animated mainly by his highly developed sensitivity. From the very beginning he sees himself as a sensitive soul at the mercy of his natural environment; his love fills him with 'a gentle ecstasy which absorbs the entire duration' of his happiness and 'gathers it together into a point like that of eternity'. Yet, because 'this eternity of happiness was only a moment in his life' (II, 317), it cannot lift him permanently above the psychological limitations of human love, especially when he is the victim of a 'heated' imagination which, like that of Jean-Jacques himself, carries everything to extremes. All his efforts to transform the 'devouring fire' of his 'ardent passion' into a 'pure' and 'divine' element cannot prevent it from being partially debased by sexual desire.

For the most part it is Julie — rather than Saint-Preux — who speaks of the purity of their love and of the 'divine fire which purifies their natural inclinations' (II, 138). Although she too has 'a sensitive soul', it soon becomes clear that her manner of loving is not the same as Saint-Preux's. This is not only because of the obvious differences of sexual psychology (a familiar item in Rousseau's didactic works), but also because of the needs of her own particular temperament. In the first place, if Saint-Preux's passion is that of a man without roots, she is the member of an intimate social and family group which has a determining influence upon her conception of love. If she succumbs to her lover's passion and seems for a time to share it, there is a side of her nature which makes her react strongly against the brutal reality of sex. One of her favourite words is 'innocence'. 'The harmony of love and innocence', she says, 'seems to me to be paradise on earth' (II, 51). True love, in Julie's opinion, rises above sexual desire and perhaps cannot be reconciled with it. 'Two months' experience', she tells Saint-

Preux before her 'fall', 'have taught me that my too tender heart has need of love but my senses have no need of a lover.' She goes on to point out that the 'moment of possession' creates a 'crisis for love' by introducing a 'dangerous element of change'. Later on she refers to a 'calm and tender love which speaks to the heart without stirring the senses' (II, 236). In view of this it is not surprising to find Saint-Preux addressing her as a 'cold and mysterious lover'. Julie does not want passionate involvement but 'peaceful, lasting enjoyment'.

This psychological factor, however, is at first not important enough to affect her desire to marry Saint-Preux. She is supported by her cousin and confidante, Claire, who vainly tries to persuade Baron d'Etange to yield to Julie's wishes. Meanwhile, another friend appears — an English aristocrat called Lord Edward Bomston who also tries (again in vain) to make the baron change his mind. In any case, the latter, whatever his attitude towards Saint-Preux's inferior social status, has already promised his daughter's hand to an old friend, M. de Wolmar, to whom he is under a great obligation. Lord Edward persists in his efforts on the young couple's behalf and even suggests that they should elope to England where he offers them a home on his estates in Yorkshire, but Julie's feelings for her parents are too strong to allow her to take advantage of his generosity.

So great is Julie's determination to force her father's consent that she lets herself be made pregnant by Saint-Preux. Unfortunately she not only has a miscarriage, but her resolution is undermined by her mother's death, for which she imagines herself — though quite mistakenly — to be responsible. Her father finally overcomes her resistance when he abandons threats and force for a desperate appeal to her feelings as a daughter, and these triumph over love; after obtaining Saint-Preux's consent, Julie marries Wolmar, convinced that she must put her duty to her parents before her passion for her lover.

Although she suffers from a strong sense of guilt and the feeling of being 'contemptible', 'unhappy' and 'guilty', she is convinced that her passion for Saint-Preux has 'degraded rather than corrupted her'; she is 'guilty but not depraved' (II, 344); her essential goodness — like that of Jean-Jacques himself — has not been destroyed. She knows that 'her heart is made for virtue and that she cannot be happy without it' (III, 344). Since innocence and love have always been necessary to her, she can never forget the 'peace and innocence' of a 'gentle even life' undisturbed by violent passion; she is constantly drawn to 'that happy time when she led an innocent, well-behaved life beneath her parents' eyes' (II, 114). Even after falling in love with Saint-Preux, she likes to dwell on 'these times of happiness and innocence when this lively and gentle fire by which we were animated purified all our feelings . . . when desires themselves seemed to be born only to give us the honour of overcoming them and of being all the worthier of each other' (II, 352). She recognizes that she has been dominated by her 'too tender heart' which will henceforth not be enough to protect her against weakness; she now needs *la sagesse* capable of bringing peace and stability to her whole being.

It is during the marriage ceremony that she suddenly becomes aware of her real inner needs and first recognizes the religious implications of her whole attitude. She makes several references to the 'sudden' and 'happy revolution' which then took place within her; 'an unknown power' corrected the 'disorder of her affections and re-established them in accordance with duty and nature'. Although she still loves Saint-Preux, it is no longer in the same way, for her soul has been purified; her senses are calm and she now feels no shame. She has at last achieved 'a new serenity' and a new being. 'I felt myself being reborn'. It is as though God has removed a veil from her eyes and 'given her back to herself in spite of herself' (II, 355-6). A 'secret voice' recalls her to 'the order of nature' and henceforth, instead of being at the mercy of her unpredictable and sensitive heart, she can rely on her steadfast will. Will and reason have strengthened her moral self by making her conscious of 'an inner effigy' which reproduces God's spiritual reality within herself; she now has 'a divine model', the 'true model of perfections' which, by offering her a glimpse of 'immutable truth', will serve as her guide (II, 358). 'It is through the contemplation of this divine model', she declares, 'that the soul is purified and elevated.' 'Sound reason' emerges at last as 'a divine torch' that lights the way to virtue and happiness. Unlike the sensibility which perishes with the vicissitudes of time, this process of purification brings security and peace to her soul. Since she also has the feeling of being reborn, she is now 'like a new being recently come forth from nature's hands' (II, 364). Perhaps in all this Julie has only become what she always wanted to be, but because the harrowing experience of an unhappy passion has not corrupted her essential being, her life can now express a goodness and virtue which will give her new strength and prepare her for a major role in the lives of those around her.

From this point onwards Julie will not be a single, clearly defined individual; she will incarnate several aspects of womanhood., It is one of the curious features of the work that the characters tend to assume multiple roles and, for Saint-Preux-Rousseau, they are never free from a certain ambiguity. A striking illustration of this is Saint-Preux's emotional reaction to Julie immediately after their first night of intimacy: he sees her as the embodiment of all possible relations with women — 'O my charming mistress, my wife, my sister, my sweet friend' (II, 149). After her marriage, Julie is treated as a source of emotional power rather than of sexual fulfilment: she is the emanation of a vital and in some ways mysterious influence which nobody can resist. For example, she inspires an intense affection in her friend Claire who, in spite of being a wife and mother, subordinates her whole being to Julie and derives the meaning of her life from this friendship. 'You subjugate me,' she confesses, 'your genius crushes mine.' 'You are meant to rule. Your sway is absolute.' Julie has 'this communicative soul which loves to diffuse itself'; the power of her 'expansive soul' which spreads 'an invincible charm upon everything around her' makes the other characters speak of her 'invincible ascendancy'. As Claire strikingly puts it: 'your heart animates all those who surround it and gives them so to speak a new being to which they are forced to do homage' (II, 409). 'All that approaches you is compelled to be like you', says Saint-Preux (II, 585). Nobody can escape her 'despotic rule', and it is appropriate that Lord Bomston should treat her like a queen ruling over 'an entire people which loves her' (II, 607).

In spite of her frequent references to the need for virtue,

Julie tends to remain identified with the principle of sensibility; it is not the austere morality of the virtuous individual but the natural goodness of the loving and loved woman which is the source of her influence. At times there seems to be an affinity between her own character and the physical nature with which she comes into contact. As a girl she enjoys 'the rural simplicity' of pleasant landscapes adorned by 'the tender cares of a common mother'. 'It is only there that one is under her auspices and can listen to her laws.' Saint-Preux also responds to the attraction of such a scene. 'I find the countryside more cheerful, the verdure fresher and more vivid, the air purer and the sky more serene ... A secret charm beautifies every object or fascinates my senses.' It is a perfect setting for a happy lover who is provided with 'a nuptial bed worthy of the beauty he adores and the fire which consumes him' (II, 116). Equally revealing is the 'Elysium' or natural garden which Julie later creates at Clarens. As Saint-Preux expresses his delight and astonishment at a corner of nature which reminds him of the remote islands he visited during his voyage round the world, Julie assures him that 'nature has done everything, but under her direction and that there is nothing that she has not arranged'. 'Everything is green, fresh and vigorous and the gardener's hand is not visible' (II, 472, 478). In spite of her art, they are still in the presence of 'an animated and sensitive nature', perfectly attuned to the needs of her own being. The very form of this 'Elysium' shows that the fresh spontaneous character of the innocent young woman is now replaced by the controlled but still unspoilt character of the virtuous wife and mother who has successfully retained her *sensibilité*.

Because of the overriding influence of 'a too tender heart which sometimes fears to punish itself for its weakness', Julie recognizes that she needs someone to provide her with moral strength. It is to her husband, the fifty-year-old M. de Wolmar, that she turns for this support. This aristocrat of Russian origin who always seems somewhat remote from everyday reality has 'a calm soul and cold heart' which, though unable to match Julie's 'goodness' and 'tenderness' (as he recognizes), provides her with 'reason' and 'order' and brings understanding and stability to her life. Exerting a powerful influence on all around him, he himself remains unchanged by people and events. His love of order, however, makes him a natural representative of virtue, for Rousseau himself constantly stresses the link between the two principles. At times Wolmar is invested with an almost divine omniscience, and on one occasion he is explicitly compared to God! (This point is in no way invalidated by the surprising announcement that, in spite of his moral rectitude, he is an atheist, for his atheism was introduced into the novel at a stage when Rousseau was striving to reconcile the *dévots* and the *philosophes*.) He is endowed with an irresistible capacity for penetrating the human soul and is identified with the image of a 'living eye'. He loves to read into men's hearts. 'If I could change the nature of my being', he asserts, 'and become a living eye, I would willingly make this change.' He has 'an almost supernatural gift of seeing into people's hearts'. If he is God, however, he is God the father too, for his paternal role is frequently emphasised throughout the novel.

While Julie admits her dependence on him — and this leads her to the surprising admission that Wolmar is really the husband she needs and that if she had to choose again, she would still prefer Wolmar to anyone else — he too recognizes his dependence on her. Virtue and reason alone cannot bring happiness and it is his wife's goodness which adds warmth and affection to his existence. In the case of the weak Saint-Preux, who is nothing when left to his own resources, the situation is quite different: as soon as he realises that Julie cannot be his, he decides to leave Europe for a long voyage round the world with Admiral Anson. On his return he receives a short letter from M. de Wolmar inviting him to live at Clarens, where he will find 'friendship, hospitality, esteem and confidence' in a house noteworthy for its 'innocence and peace'. It is soon evident, however, as Claire (who, after being married and widowed, now lives with Julie) explains, that this offer of a 'house, friendship and counsel' has been made with the intention of 'curing' Saint-Preux of his guilty passion; for, until this has been done, nobody can be perfectly happy. Wolmar, therefore, proposes to treat Saint-Preux as a sick person who has to be put through a series of tests which will eventually restore him to health and happiness and give him a 'new being' — in particular, by showing him that the Julie de

Wolmar whom he believes he loves is no longer the young Julie d'Etange of the past, Wolmar hopes to strengthen Saint-Preux with the force of virtue. Wolmar's greatest achievement will be to let Saint-Preux find a 'peace of soul' which is the condition of all lasting happiness. Saint-Preux himself will be made to realize that he is no longer 'an ordinary man' but a 'strong and noble soul' worthy of those who are giving him their esteem and friendship. As far as Wolmar is concerned, however, he remains a child and is constantly treated as such. Indeed, Saint-Preux himself is quite ready to accept this role and he comes to see himself as 'the child of the house'; he tells Wolmar: 'I was dead to virtue as well as to happiness; I owe you this moral life to which I feel myself being reborn. O my benefactor! O my father! By giving myself entirely to you, I can offer you, as to God himself, only the gifts which I hold from you' (II, 611). Always conscious of Wolmar's watchful eye, this 'weak and frail' man cannot stand alone; he tells Julie that 'it is only near her that he is safe against himself' (II, 678). She gives him psychological support, just as Wolmar gives him moral support. The esteem which is also necessary to his peace of mind is provided by his friend Lord Edward Bomston who treats him as an equal, even though Saint-Preux cannot help seeing himself as his 'friend, creature and pupil'. When at last he has become 'a sublime and pure soul triumphing over its passions and holding sway over itself', he can consider himself the equal of those 'great and strong souls' who constitute the company of the elect.

This greatness of soul is not achieved without difficulty, and Saint-Preux has to prove himself in several 'tests'. When, for example, during Wolmar's absence, he and Julie take a boat-trip across the lake and visit Meillerie, where he had spent 'such sad and delightful days' thinking of her, he cannot help reminding her of the past. With Julie's help, however, he resists the temptation to try to relive it and is 'completely given back to himself', being made fully aware of 'man's freedom and the merit of virtue'.

In spite of the stress on emotional conflict, the second half of the novel shows that personal relations have to be integrated into social and communal life. Wolmar and his wife are not only individuals in their own right, but also the lords and masters of the society of Clarens, and into his description of this society Rousseau has undoubtedly projected some of his favourite social aspirations. Yet, as scholars have shown, this superior world is a subtle combination of fantasy and realism, for Rousseau drew freely on many contemporary accounts of provincial life as well as upon his own imagination.[2] Nevertheless, the picture which eventually emerges is of a community shaped and guided by principles very close to the author's own heart, and is in some ways similar to the communal life described at the end of *Emile*. If the house occupied by the masters is seen as the 'temple of virtue', it is also remarkable for its innocence and peace. 'Peace', 'serenity', 'rest' and 'security' — these are the words frequently used to describe an abode that in many ways possesses 'all the charms of the golden age' (II, 603). Needless to say,Clarens gives Rousseau an excellent opportunity of extolling the life of the countryside at the expense of depressing city life — a point which is given particular emphasis by Saint-Preux's critical description of Paris when he spends some time in the capital. During his stay he becomes a shrewd and critical observer of urban society, summarising his views in a passage which has a very modern resonance: 'It is the first disadvantage of large towns that men become there other than what they are and society gives them so to speak a being different from their own. This is true and especially in Paris, and in relation to women who draw from other people's look 'the only existence about which they care' (II, 273).

The peace and innocence of the rural community of Clarens rest upon the secure foundations of 'order' and 'rule'. Since order is the guiding principle of Wolmar's own life, it is not surprising that 'a well-ordered house is the image of the master's soul' and that Saint-Preux should speak of 'the admirable order which prevails there' (II, 450, 466). Order, peace, innocence — these are the characteristics of Clarens. At the same time the members of this stable and united community have a strong sense of sharing a common purpose. 'A small number of gentle, peaceful people, united by mutual needs and a reciprocal benevolence contribute by various cares to a common end' (II, 547). This intimate and happy community respects human dignity and freedom. 'Man', says

83

Julie, 'is too noble a being to serve simply as an instrument for other people' and 'it is never permissible to degrade a human soul for the advantage of others' (II, 536).

Yet this freedom is not that of social equals, for Clarens, as many critics have observed, is a strictly paternalistic, hierarchical community. All authority, though willingly accepted, comes from above. Mme de Wolmar 'does not favour changes in condition' and everyone remains in his allotted place (II, 536). The masters, however, look upon themselves as parents and upon their servants as children. Even the sexes are strictly separated (again in accordance with one of Rousseau's favourite ideas) and this separation allegedly contributes to the stability of the community. Everything takes place beneath the watchful gaze of masters, who are treated as parents and gods.

It is not necessary to give a detailed account of the economic organization of this society which, relying on agriculture rather than on trade, tries to be as self-sufficient as possible. Clarens is a kind of island which seeks to be independent of the rest of the world. The house is the focal point of the community, but it exists in an agreeable natural setting which not only gives it beauty and charm but also helps to provide it with an active and productive life. As far as Saint-Preux is concerned, it is a 'society after his own heart', but, seen in a still broader perspective, it is a microcosm reflecting the essential order and unity of nature herself. 'Everything converges on the common good in the universal system. Every man has his place in the best order of things; it is a question of finding this place and of not perverting this order' (II, 563).

In this paternalistic society fulfilment seems to assume two different forms, for the masters and their servants do not enjoy the same kind of happiness. The self-realization of the 'great and noble souls' is vividly illustrated by the remarkable episode of *la matinée à l'anglaise*, which portrays one of the most important themes of the work — the need to find 'this openness of heart which puts all feelings, all thoughts in common, and makes each one, as he feels himself to be what he ought to be, show himself to all as he is' (II, 689). Saint-Preux, in particular, is attracted by the thought that he no longer needs to conceal anything from his friends; he is happy to feel that 'there remains nothing in the depths of our hearts which we wish to hide from one another' (II, 557). He will now 'dare to show himself' to Wolmar, for he is sustained by 'a new elevation'. The *matinée à l'anglaise* describes an idyllic moment when the friends have withdrawn from the rest of the community in order to enjoy the closest intimacy. 'We want to be recollected (*recueillis*) so to speak in one another.' The moment of supreme happiness is reached when the three friends remain in a state of 'motionless ecstasy' and are absorbed by a 'universal self-communion'. Such an experience has no need of words or other outward sign. As Saint-Preux rather curiously puts it, they wish to be 'without a witness in order to be able to say nothing to each other at their ease'. The presence of a single stranger would destroy the charm of this perfect personal communion. Such a high level of experience is possible only to those exceptional souls who have known how to appreciate the feelings of 'sensitive men'.

Characteristically, the communal event expressing the spirit of Clarens takes place out-of-doors and, unlike the con-templative rapture of the *matinée à l'anglaise*, is a scene of joyous participation; everybody is busy with activities in which work is barely distinguishable from play. The occasion is *la fête des vendanges*, or the wine-harvest, in which the whole of Clarens takes part. The mood is very similar to that of the happy entertainment which Rousseau envisaged for the Genevans in the *Letter to d'Alembert*. Amid the 'simplicity of pastoral and country life' are to be found 'all the charms of the golden age' and a 'general gladness which seems to extend over the face of the earth'. The scene is reminiscent of the Biblical age as everybody is 'transported to the times of the patriarchs'. This 'time of love and innocence' recalls the shy affection of Rachel or the gentleness of Naomi. 'No, never does beauty hold greater sway than in the midst of rural cares' (II, 604). Appropriately, too, the happy workers express their feelings through song and dance. There is a 'concert of voices' singing in unison, while human voices mingle with 'the hoarse sound of rustic instruments'. As the *fête* ends with a display of fireworks, everybody is content with 'a day spent in work, gaiety, innocence and would not be sorry to begin again on the morrow, the day after that and his whole life through' (II, 611).

The novel does not end on this note of happy communal

fulfilment, for its last parts pay increasing attention to the subject of religion, and, in this respect, they may be compared and contrasted with the views expressed in the *Profession of Faith*; but whereas the *Profession* discusses the principles of natural religion as applicable to all men of good faith, the religious issue of *La Nouvelle Héloïse* tends to be limited to the character of Julie. Although the 'profession de foi' made by the dying Julie corresponds very largely to Rousseau's own views, her personal reactions elsewhere do not necessarily command the author's unqualified approval, for they are connected with the theme of love and virtue as imaginatively elaborated in the novel. It is clear that the closely-knit, self-sufficient society of Clarens, with its air of security and permanence, does not exclude an element of dissatisfaction which becomes particularly obvious in the development of Julie's character. At first sight she seems to be a completely fulfilled woman — as wife, mother and friend. 'I see nothing that does not extend my being,' she declares, 'and nothing that divides it; it is in all around me, there is no part of it that is far from me; my imagination has nothing more to do, I have nothing more to desire: to feel and to enjoy are for me the same thing; I live in all that I love; I am satiated with life and happiness' (II, 689). Yet this expression of perfect fulfilment is followed by the striking statement that 'happiness bores her'. She is suffering from *ennui* and a 'secret langour steals into the depths of my heart, which I feel to be empty and dilated'. It soon emerges that her happiness runs counter to a fundamental human need: to love is to desire. 'Woe to him who has nothing more to desire! He loses so to speak all he possesses. People derive less enjoyment from what they obtain than from what they hope for, and they are happy only before they are happy!' She adds that 'the land the chimeras is the only one worth living in; such is the nothingness of human affairs that, apart from the Being who exists through himself, there is nothing beautiful save what is not' (II, 693). To ignore or to suppress desire is to deny the power of the imagination which always tends to go beyond active achievement and impel the individual to renewed effort. Secreted in imagination and desire is a need for the absolute, which no finite activity can fully satisfy and this is why Julie, after indulging in a mood of contemplative mysticism, turns more and more to the thought of the next world.

The way in which man's aspiration to perfection always involves an element of unreality is also stressed in Rousseau's analysis of love in *Emile*. After pointing out that love is impossible without 'enthusiasm', he affirms: 'there is no enthusiasm without an object of perfection, whether real or imaginary, but always existing in the imagination. All is illusion in love, but what is real are the feelings it inspires in us for the true beauty which it makes us love. This beauty is not in the loved object but is the product of our errors. But what does it matter? Are people any less willing to sacrifice all base feelings to this imaginary model?' (IV, 743). Towards the end of *Emile* he returns to the same point when he mentions the relationship between imagination and beauty. 'Imagination which adorns what is desired abandons it at the moment of possession. Except for the sole Being who exists by himself, there is nothing beautiful save what is not. If this state could have lasted for ever, you would have found supreme happiness' (IV, 821).

Perhaps it is the thought of love's ephemeral or unattainable aspects which explains the increasing emphasis upon the idea of death in *La Nouvelle Héloïse*. It had already made a brief appearance in the passionate phase of Julie's relationship with Saint-Preux. After his first night with her he had written: 'O let us die, my sweet friend, let us die, my heart's beloved. What can we do henceforth with an insipid youth of which we have exhausted all the delights?' (II, 147). Julie also speaks of the 'langour of death' which follows the extinction of love. It is very remarkable how, after describing the satiety of her happiness, she exclaims: 'O death, come when you will! I fear you no more, I have lived, I have forestalled you, I have no more feelings to know, you have nothing more to take from me' (II 689). Now that all the possibilities of her being have been fulfilled, she feels that her life will merely decline, or else court disaster by dwelling on the one feeling which she has so far successfully overcome — her passion for Saint-Preux. Death will solve this problem by taking her to eternity. From this point of view her death at the end of the novel may not be very different from a form of suicide, even though she actually dies as a result of rescuing one of her children from drowning.

Her last pathetic letter to Saint-Preux (which is delivered to him only after her death) shows that she still fears the future, in spite of her belief that 'her virtue remains spotless and her love without remorse' (II, 741).

Her death ensures the permanence of her sway, for now that she is beyond their reach, the other characters can truly feel that they are 'her work' and that her heart 'remains in their midst'. Moreover, the survivors will be brought closer together by their adoration of the dead woman. Wolmar himself, hitherto isolated by his atheism, will in due course be won over to religious faith, and by her death Julie will be able to achieve what was impossible in her lifetime. Saint-Preux, who has already been warned by the devoted Claire that no man who loved Julie could ever be her own husband, will become the eternal bachelor devoting himself to Julie's family and yet fortified by the knowledge that the virtue which separated them on earth will unite them in heaven. Julie's last words are to say that she is 'too happy to buy at the cost of my life the right to love you for ever without crime and to tell you so once more' (II, 743).

The novel seems to describe what may be called in Kierkega-ardian terms three 'stages of existence'. Its early parts portray the period of idealistic passion, showing how this can be stifled or destroyed by the powerful influence of social prejudice as well as by some of its own psychological tensions and complexities; self-centred erotic love then gives way to a social and moral ideal expressed through the life of an orderly and well-organised community; finally, the ideal society of Clarens is disrupted by the death of one of its 'great souls', for Julie feels impelled to move on to a religious experience which cannot find satisfaction in the life immediately available to her but requires the ultimate reality of life-after-death. Perhaps none of these stages is conceivable without the others, but it is made clear that the striving for happiness constantly encounters obstacles which cause a man to move forward in search of new ideals, even though these may be expressed only in term of absence or negation. In other words, the activity of the imagination, which Rousseau carefully controls in works aimed at providing mankind with principles of universal validity, shows that these principles can be fraught with considerable difficulty and danger when they are expressed in the lives of individuals living in particular situations. In this respect, therefore, Rousseau's novel, while not formally repudiating the didactic principles elaborated elsewhere, throws into relief the power of emotions and impulses which will be given even more forceful expression in personal writings concerned not with imaginary characters but with the real being of Jean-Jacques himself.

5. The New Citizen

The concluding sections of such works as *Emile* and the *Letter to d'Alembert*, as well as the later part of *La Nouvelle Héloïse*, reveal Rousseau's attempts to imagine an ideal society freed from the constraints and defects of existing civilization. He was obviously attracted by the picture of a closed, almost self-sufficient community that combined the acceptance of order with the enjoyment of spontaneous emotions. Although such a community was essentially paternalistic, its members were open to one another and able to indulge in the uninhibited expression of their own — and one another's — feelings. Individual and collective needs were perfectly balanced, for the experience of personal happiness was inseparable from the consciousness of contributing to the common good. That is why communal activities — involving either play or work — occupy such a large place in the life of such communities. At the same time stability and security depend on the wisdom of the 'great souls' who show a watchful concern for the well-being of the society and its members. Yet such wisdom is not felt to be oppressive since it serves to make everyone aware of the natural goodness which is already 'engraved in his heart in indelible characters'.

Rousseau recognizes that such societies are exceptional and that modern man has to live in a different kind of environment; he must accept the need for political institutions whose principles owe more to reason than to feeling and imagination. Any thinker concerned with the philosophy of human nature is obliged to produce a rational solution to the problem of man's involvement with his fellows. Quite early on in his career Rousseau had given serious thought to this matter and in the *Confessions* he tell us that he planned to write an extensive work called *Political Institutions*. Although it was never completed, the project played an important part in his work as a whole. Political issues become all the more important when we recall Rousseau's emphasis upon the decisive role of government in most men's lives. 'I had seen that everything was radically dependent on politics and that, however one set about it, no nation would ever be anything except what the nature of its government made it be' (I, 404).

Rousseau was given his first serious opportunity for developing his thoughts on political matters when Diderot invited him to write the article 'Political Economy' for the *Encyclopaedia*. This eventually appeared in the fifth volume published in April 1755. It is obvious, therefore, that Rousseau was already pondering political theory at the time when he was preparing the *Discourse on Inequality*. As well as leading him to put forward ideas such as the distinction between sovereignty and government, and the concept of the general will, the article gave particular prominence to the view that society is not a simple extension of 'nature' but a form of organised life that runs counter in many ways to nature in the primitive sense.

This stress upon the difference between nature and political society, though essential to Rousseau's thought (it will reappear in the *Social Contract*), was not new. All the thinkers of the Natural Law School accepted the idea of society as originating in human conventions. The different conclusions drawn from this premise (for example, Hobbes was a supporter of political absolutism while Locke defended the liberal position) in no way affected their conviction that paternal power and civil power were quite different; they were firmly opposed to Filmer (the author of *Patriarcha*) and Bossuet who had identified fathers with rulers. The essential point for Locke and Hobbes was that society had been brought into being by a deliberate act of choice on the part of men who believed they were acting for their own advantage. The fact that, historically, they failed to achieve their aim in no way affected the validity of the principle or its rational intention. Admittedly, Rousseau does not explicitly mention the idea of the social contract in the article on 'Political Economy', but he is there concerned with 'the fundamental rule of government' and the essential nature of political authority, not with its origin and history. A properly constituted political order forms an 'organised living body', with its various parts having the same essential functions as those of the human body. It ought to be controlled by a main principle — the general will aimed at the preservation and happiness of each part; this general will, the fundamental rule of government, is the basis of the laws by which all citizens obey the same 'rule of justice', thus subordinating selfish interests, whether those of individuals or of groups, to the requirements of the public good. It follows that 'the most general will is always the most just and that the voice of the people is indeed the voice of God' (III, 246). Moreover, the law, like the general will sustaining it, is always concerned with the general well-being and seeks to assure 'the goods, life and freedom of each member by the protection of all' (III, 248). Without such a law and 'this celestial voice which dictates to each citizen the precepts of public reason and teaches him to act according to the maxims of his own judgement and not to be in contradiction with himself', it would be impossible for men to know freedom and justice.

A further point emphasised by the article is that the true basis of political authority is not mere obedience. 'The most absolute authority is that which penetrates man's inner being and operates as much upon his will as upon his actions' (III, 251). A durable political society will consist of men who love the laws and do not merely obey them. This was a secret well understood by ancient governments. Moreover, if members of society are to contribute to the common good by following the general will, they must recognize the need for virtue, for virtue is only 'this conformity of the particular will to the general'. In short, the wise legislator will realise that 'the mainspring of public authority is in the hearts of the citizens and that nothing can make up for morals (*moeurs*) in the maintenance of government'. Every sound state needs good, honest people if it is to survive: those who ignore the force of moral feelings and principles in their private lives are likely to become immoral and criminal in their social attitudes. Rousseau is here affirming a point affecting his entire political philosophy and one that is given emphatic expression in *Emile*: 'those who wish to separate politics and morality will never understand anything of either' (IV, 524).

Sound political institutions, therefore, must satisfy the requirements of reason and morality; they will rely on intelligent self-interest to ensure the physical survival and well-being of the community, and at the same time they will exert a moral influence by encouraging citizens to fulfil the highest possibilities of their existence. Since it permeates the inner lives of the citizens, political society is of a decisive importance; 'peoples are in the long run what the government makes them — warriors, citizens, men when it wishes, populace and rabble when it pleases' (III, 251). Because no community can survive for long without the willing cooperation of its members, it is important to engender the appropriate sentiments in the citizens' hearts. This is why, in Rousseau's opinion, patriotism is so important. *La patrie* is not some impersonal objective entity but a 'common' and 'tender mother' who unites freedom with virtue. Since Rousseau was full of enthusiasm for Geneva when he was writing his article, praising it as a place where 'liberty was established, the government calm, the citizens enlightened, firm and modest, knowing and bravely maintaining their rights', it is not surprising that he stresses the importance of this theme. He insists that 'the greatest marvels of virtue have been produced by the love of the fatherland'; 'this sweet and lively feeling which joins the force of pride to all the beauty of virtue, gives it an energy which, without disfiguring it, makes it the most heroic of all the passions' (III, 255). In a burst of lyrical eloquence Rousseau extols patriotism as one of man's noblest impulses. 'Do you want nations to be happy? Then begin by making them love their country.' Yet patriotism must animate and be animated by other moral impulses. 'The fatherland cannot survive without freedom, nor freedom without virtue, nor virtue without the citizens.' This ideal will be achieved as soon as the citizens identify themselves with a reality greater than their own and come to love their fatherland with a 'sublime virtue' worthy of 'this great object'. This means that patriotism will permeate all aspects of national life. As Rousseau was to write in a letter some years later: 'It is neither walls nor men who make up the fatherland; it is the laws, the manners, the customs, the government, the constitution, the mode of being which results from all that'. The fatherland is inseparable from the relations of the State to its members: when 'the relations change or are destroyed, the fatherland vanishes' (*CC*, XIX, 190).

Yet patriotism is impossible without effective education. Since citizens cannot be formed in a day, it is necessary to begin at a very early age by making all members of the community 'identify themselves in some way with the great whole, feel themselves to be members of the fatherland and constantly raise their souls to this great object'. A stable and patriotic community will accord a high place to public education. Already we can discern Rousseau's strong predilection for the compact, closely integrated society in which all citizens feel close to the community and to one another. 'Wherever a people loves its country, respects the laws and lives simply, little remains to be done to make it happy' (III, 262).

Although the *Encyclopaedia* article provides a useful introduction to Rousseau's political philosophy, it is only in the *Social Contract* of 1762 that he produced a more detailed elaboration of his ideas. Even that work, as we have seen and as Rousseau himself indicates in his foreword, was part of a much larger treatise, the *Political Institutions,* which he had 'formerly undertaken without having considered his strength and which had long since been abandoned'. The *Social Contract,* however, remains 'the most considerable fragment and the one least unworthy of being offered to the public'.

For some time it was not unusual for critics to see *Emile* and the *Social Contract* as contradictory works, the former being treated as an exposition of 'individualism' and the latter as that of 'collectivism'.[1] Such, however, was clearly not Rousseau's view — and the previous analysis will already have shown the inadequacy of such terms to describe Rousseau's thought — for he insisted that the two works were but parts of a single whole. Moreover, it would have been very odd for him to include a summary of his political treatise in the last book of *Emile* if he had believed the two works to be irreconcilable. It has already been pointed out that the ultimate purpose of *Emile* was not to produce an individual existing apart from other men but one whose moral maturity would make it possible for him to become a responsible member of society. Emile realises that personal happiness is unobtainable without the self-control and virtue which will allow him to overcome inclination for the sake of duty. This cannot be effectively achieved until he learns to adapt himself to a social order that is not imposed upon him by the arbitrary will of other people but is the expression of his own inner being. For this to become possible the individual will have to live in society and relate his existence to that of his fellows.

The close link between morality and politics is strengthened by Rousseau's emphasis upon the principle of necessity, henceforth transformed from the physical form it had assumed in Emile's early education into a more human and moral one. Whether man is living in the presence of physical nature or in the company of his fellow-men, he has to recognize the reality of his dependence on some kind of inescapable necessity. Rousseau, therefore, proposes to give it a political form that will have the same limiting yet liberating functions as its physical counterpart.

'There are two kinds of dependence: dependence on things, which belongs to nature; dependence on men, which belongs to society. Dependence on things, having no morality, is not harmful to freedom and does not engender vices; dependence on men, being uncontrolled, engenders them all, and it is through this dependence that master and slave become mutually depraved. If there is some means of curing this evil in society, it is through substituting law for men and arming the general wills with a real strength that is superior to the influence of any particular will. If the laws of nations could have, like those of nature, an inflexibility which no human force would ever overcome, dependence on men would again become dependence on things: in the commonwealth all the advantages of the natural state would be combined with those of the civil state; to the freedom which keeps men exempt from vice would be added the morality which lifts them up to virtue' (IV, 311).

Yet virtue means the fulfilment of the self, not its destruction or mutilation, and no individual can be expected to become virtuous at the cost of denying his essential nature. Although virtue may require the sacrifice of inclination, it has to be consistent with man's need for freedom. In the same way the ideal society will not be a purely restrictive one, for the very limitations it imposes on the arbitrary exercise of force are intended to protect the freedom of its members. Moreover, virtue and freedom are not merely abstract concepts but have to be related to the demands of everyday life, so that every citizen must be given security and protection as well as opportunities for moral fulfilment. Valid political constitutions, therefore, must respect that most fundamental of human attributes — 'self-love' — which involves all essential aspects of man's being, including the desire for self-preservation. At the very beginning of the *Social Contract*, Rousseau points out that, even though he proposes to discuss the laws as they 'can be', he is prepared to take 'men as they are'; he will always try to combine 'what right permits with what interest prescribes, so that justice and utility are not divided'.

Sound political thought thus has to accept the basic needs of human nature and at the same time allow for its moral possibilities. More especially, there are certain requirements of 'natural law' which form part of every man's life and have to be respected by both philosophers and rulers; God and nature have laid down limits beyond which man cannot go, and any thinker who ignores this fact is indulging in utopian fantasy and producing a political constitution that has no relevance to real life. Although, as we shall see, 'natural law' in its highest form involves a transformation of its primitive elements and is not to be equated with the 'natural freedom' of primitive man, the sub-title of the *Social Contract* — 'principles of political right' — shows that the work is presenting a radical challenge to the existing order, for Rousseau is concerned more with what ought to be than with what actually is; he sees himself pursuing an aim quite different from that of his illustrious predecessor Montesquieu. Whereas the latter was interested in the analysis of real governments and laws with a view to understanding the mechanism of political and legal life in its historical and physical context, Rousseau's concern with 'right' makes him consider constitutions as they ought to be. Admittedly, in many places he pays heed to the lessons of Montesquieu's *Spirit of the Laws* — especially when he comes to consider the relevance of particular situations and circumstances to the application of universal political principles — but he is also at pains to stress his own special purpose, insisting that 'political right has yet to be reborn'. 'The only modern writer capable of creating this great and useless (*sic*) science would have been the illustrious Montesquieu, but he took care not to treat questions of political right; he contented

himself with treating the positive right of established governments; and there is nothing in the world more different than
these two studies' (IV 836).

In spite of Rousseau's sever criticism of his predecessors'
work in the field of natural right, it is clear that his ultimate
intention is not essentially different from theirs, for they too
had been concerned with establishing 'right' rather than fact.
In this respect Montesquieu had been more original, for he had
sought to examine governments in a scientific spirit or at least
to explain how they had come about through the laws of cause
and effect. Admittedly, he had started off with a metaphysical
assumption about the relationship of laws to the 'nature of
things', but this had not prevented him from analysing the
problem with a view to determining the causes that had
produced laws and government and had given them their
existing characteristics. Rousseau too is not unaware of the
need to relate his ideas to political reality, but he is concerned
primarily with the principles by which the validity of that
reality can be judged. The main burden of his attack, therefore,
is not directed against Montesquieu but against those earlier
thinkers who, in his view, had been seriously mistaken in their
ideas and attitude. What he finds particularly reprehensible is
the way in which his predecessors had allowed their principles
to be perverted by their subservience to existing authority. In
this respect Rousseau sees himself as a writer whose idealism
refuses to let him stoop to unworthy compromises of this kind.
He had already taken issue with the Dutch jurist Grotius in the
Discourse on Inequality on the question of natural right and
man's condition in the state of nature. Now, however, he taxes
him not merely with error but with deliberate bad faith,
insisting that he had wanted to curry favour with his patrons
by reasoning 'from fact to right' in a way that was 'favourable
to tyrants'.

One particular point stressed by predecessors such as
Grotius and Puffendorf, and one that Rousseau finds extremely repugnant, is the idea that there are 'natural slaves'.
Rousseau insists that, if men who are born to slavery lose their
desire to be anything else, this is simply due to a passive
acceptance of their position. 'Force made the first slaves,
cowardice has perpetuated them'. It is impossible, affirms

Rousseau, to establish any right by means of force, for no man has any natural authority over others.

In the first version of the *Social Contract*, the argument was reinforced by a chapter ('On the Society of Mankind') which was omitted from the published work. As well as taking up a point already made in the *Encyclopaedia* article, 'Political Economy', which had established a basic distinction between natural and conventional authority, this chapter is undoubtedly related to another article in the same publication, the one on 'Natural Right' which had been contributed by Rousseau's erstwhile friend, the editor-in-chief, Denis Diderot. Whereas Diderot had suggested that the origins of society might be found in some universal aspect of human nature, a kind of innate 'general will' which would make men aware of their mutual obligations to one another, Rousseau returns to the point made in his second *Discourse* — that men did not have any such notion in the state of nature because there was no communication between them. They might indeed heed 'the gentle voice of nature' in that primitive state and even enjoy 'the happy life of the golden age' with all its 'ancient innocence', but they would never have become true men if they had continued to lead an isolated and self-absorbed existence; there would have been 'no goodness in their hearts or morality in their actions' because they would never have savoured 'the most delightful feeling of the soul, which is the love of virtue'. The development of human powers, including reason, inevitably led to some diminution of natural feelings and the consequent increase in the consciousness of personal interest, so that when men eventually came together, it was not through the influence of 'natural law' in the primitive sense of the term, but through the 'law of reason'. In other words, the social contract was not 'dictated by nature' since it was a distinctively human achievement. 'Although the laws of justice and equality are nothing for those who at one and the same time live in the freedom of the state of nature and are subject to the needs of the social state, let us try to draw from the evil itself the remedy which must cure it' (III, 288). Man has to make an effort to find a mode of existence which will enable him to overcome the difficulties and limitations of communal existence, and this cannot be done without the cooperation of his reason and his will.

The *Social Contract* carries one stage further the ideas about freedom which already figure so prominently in *Emile*, but they are now examined in a specifically social and political context. At the same time Rousseau re-affirms the essentially human aspect of the principle. If all legitimate political authority must rest on a convention or an agreement of some kind, and if it is inconceivable that any mature man would accept the idea of blind obedience to absolute authority, it is because such a notion corresponds to a fundamental need of every truly moral and rational being. To suppose the contrary is to repudiate the very basis of human existence. 'To renounce one's freedom is to renounce one's condition as a man, the rights of humanity and even one's duties. There is no possible compensation for the one who renounces everything.' Such a renunciation would be incompatible with man's nature and would 'remove all morality from his actions as well as freedom from his will' (I, iv; III, 356).

The positive expression of freedom also offers man the opportunity for developing his innate powers and attaining a higher mode of existence. It will be recalled that Emile had been urged to put virtue above feeling and to direct his energies upon the general good as a means of achieving personal fulfilment. The *Social Contract* reinforces this point by suggesting that, when he follows the demands of reason and morality, man can lift himself above the level of the animals and, by passing from 'the state of nature' to the 'civil state', achieve a 'very remarkable change', for he 'substitutes justice for instinct in his behaviour and gives his actions the morality they previously lacked'. Since the 'voice of duty' replaces 'physical impulse' and 'right' replaces 'appetite', a man's nature undergoes a striking development; 'he now acts on other principles and consults his reason before listening to his inclinations'. Although he may thereby seem to have lost some of the advantages of his primitive natural condition, he acquires new benefits which greatly outweigh any such loss. 'It is moral freedom which alone makes man master of himself, for the mere impulse of appetite is slavery and obedience to the law which one has prescribed for oneself is freedom.' That the moral freedom which leads to self-mastery is not merely negative is shown by its effects upon the rest of the human personality. The first version of the *Social Contract* had already suggested that the exercise of reason and will could 'warm a man's heart with new feelings' in a way that would 'increase his being and happiness by sharing them with his fellow-men' (III, 288); the final *Social Contract* eloquently develops the same point: 'Although he is deprived in this state [i.e. society] of certain advantages which he derives from nature, he gains far greater ones: his faculties are exercised and developed, his ideas extended, his feelings enobled, while his entire soul is elevated to the point that if the abuse of this new condition did not often bring him lower than the one from which he has emerged, he ought constantly to bless the happy moment which removed him for ever from his primitive condition and transformed him from a stupid animal into an intelligent being and man' (I, viii; III, 364).

This eulogy of freedom, though expressed by Rousseau with particular force and eloquence, was in conformity with one of the main features of the Enlightenment, which had consistently striven for the preservation of freedom as the indispensable basis of human dignity. For the *philosophes* it did not have a merely intellectual value, but formed part of their commitment to humanitarian principles. Articles in the *Encyclopaedia* protested vigorously against the enslavement of the Negroes, and often in the name of a principle very similar to Rousseau's. The Chevalier de Jaucourt declared in his article, 'Traité des Nègres', that 'men and their freedom are not an object of trade; they cannot be sold, bought or paid for at any price. There is not a single one of these unfortunates whom people claim to be mere slaves who has not the right to be declared free, since he has never lost his freedom and could not lose it, and no ruler, father or anyone in the world had the right to dispose of it.' Any formal legal sanction given to slavery has no validity at all, since there is no law which gives a man the right 'to trample underfoot the laws of nature and the eternal laws of equity which bind all men at all times and in all places'. In his article 'Political Authority' Diderot had made a similar plea for freedom. 'Freedom is a present from heaven and every individual of the same species has the right to enjoy it as soon as he enjoys reason.' Government must be by consent; 'man must not and cannot give himself completely and unreservedly to another man', for he has a 'higher master' in God. A sound political society rests on 'the observation of the laws, the preservation of freedom and the law of the fatherland'. Such a society is diametrically opposed to the despotic regimes of the East; it is a 'society of men united by reason, activated by virtue and governed by an equally proud and glorious leader according to the laws of justice'. Finally, Montesquieu, in spite of his efforts to remain detached and objective in his appraisal of political institutions, was constantly praising the merits of freedom, although he usually related it to the observation of the laws. More generally still, the liberal tradition stemming from Locke stressed the need for all sound political societies to protect and encourage freedom as the individual's most important attribute.

If Rousseau's emphasis on freedom brings him close to many of the liberally minded thinkers of his time, he introduces another — and less commonly accepted — notion into his political philosophy. This is equality, which he deems to be an essential concomitant of freedom, since freedom must be for all. It is significant that the chapter which discusses the nature of the political association constantly uses the words 'each' and 'all', as is already apparent in Rousseau's formulation of the problem: 'To find a form of association which will defend with all the common force the person and goods of each associate, and through which each one, while uniting himself with all, obeys noone but himself and remains as free as before' (I, vi; III, 360). The freedom of the political association depends on conditions which are valid for all. Obedience to the community will thus be regarded by each member as obedience to principles freely chosen by himself; this means that no individual will be required to submit to conditions which are not also applicable to everyone else. Justice demands that all the members of the community enjoy equal rights and undertake the same obligations.

This equality is possible only if every individual begins by surrendering ('alienating') all his rights to the association as a whole. This surrender has to be total, for, if the individual were allowed to hold back any rights, he might be in a position to subject others to his own will; natural freedom and natural right cannot be allowed to go unchecked, for they could be transformed into instruments of injustice and inequality. For any individual to withhold any particular right would be 'to take back so much strength from the body of the State' (II, xi; III, 149). This radical step, however, is intended to be only the first stage of a process by which the individual will eventually recover certain fundamental rights protected by the force of the whole community, so that instead of retaining the precarious benefits of the 'state of nature', which depend solely on his own strength and resources, he will henceforth be able to enjoy the unassailable rights guaranteed to him by the whole body politic.

This combination of freedom and equality in the political community means that, in Rousseau's opinion, justice can be reconciled with self-interest; political right does not remain a purely abstract or altruistic principle since it appeals to the self-interest of every individual by offering him security and protection. A fundamental requirement of human nature is thus respected, for justice is reconciled with 'each man's preference for himself'. Nevertheless, the notion of self-interest, when related to the wider context of a society based on freedom and equality, involves certain inescapable consequences which would not be found in the state of nature. Having once given his consent to the 'social contract', the individual cannot be allowed to ignore it and, in a famous phrase, 'he will be forced to be free'. What Rousseau means is that no individual can be allowed to put the whole community at risk for the sake of satisfying a narrowly selfish desire; he cannot be allowed to endanger the security of others by ignoring conditions to which he, through a quite rational and deliberate act, has given his free consent. In fact, Rousseau considers that any individual who behaves in an irresponsible, anti-social way is either wicked or insane and has to be restrained from harming the community and himself. By 'forcing him to be free' the community will (it is hoped) make him heed the demands of his own true self.

Here we see a typical case of the close link between Rousseau's view of politics and morality. As a member of the political community, the individual is involved in a moral — as well as a legal — obligation to respect its principles; his status as citizen thus provides him with an opportunity of attaining personal fulfilment and maturity. In this respect Rousseau differs from a liberal thinker like Locke who treated the State as a convenient device for protecting individual rights which did not originate in society but were part of human nature from the very beginning; for Rousseau, on the other hand, citizenship means the inescapable moral involvement of the individual in the life of the community.

If Rousseau considers the State to be a freely formed association in which all members participate on equal terms by virtue of the initial 'alienation' of all their rights, he is still faced with the problem of defining the exact nature and role of the supreme power or 'common force' which is thus brought into being. The problem of sovereignty had already attracted the attention of a number of political thinkers before Rousseau. The Frenchman Jean Bodin (1530-96) had been one of the first to give it close attention in his large-scale work *On the Republic* (1576), and the problem had been taken up by subsequent thinkers, especially those of the School of Natural Right, who often connected it with the notion of the social contract. The idea of the 'sovereignty of the people' had also been developed before Rousseau and was one of the principles on which the political constitution of Geneva was supposed to rest. In practice, however, it was usually modified in accordance with political circumstances: in Geneva, for example, it was a source of controversy between the oligarchic rulers of the republic and the 'Representatives' who wanted to participate in the running of the State. Some political theorists, especially Hobbes, recognized that sovereignty originally belonged to the people but maintained that it had been handed over, by means of a second contract, to an absolute ruler who exercised it on the people's behalf: sovereignty, therefore, could be modified or transferred in accordance with particular situations and circumstances.

Rousseau firmly rejects any idea of a second contract; the only contract is the one by which the people makes itself into a political society. He states quite categorically that there should never be any question of the people handing over sovereignty to a ruler; it is a sacred trust which can never be given up by those in whom it is invested. The only way in which sovereignty can be overcome is by the dissolution of the State itself, for, when that happens, a people returns to the 'state of nature' and resumes its natural freedom. As long as it exists, sovereignty is 'inalienable, indivisible and absolute'. The sovereign, as a collective being, 'can never be represented by anyone except itself'. This is because sovereignty is 'essentially will and will is not transmitted'. As the ultimate power of the State, it cannot be given up or divided in any way. It may seem that Rousseau is here closer to Hobbes than to the liberal thinkers, for Hobbes, as a champion of absolute monarchy, defended the absolute claims of sovereignty. On the other hand, Rousseau, who gives a more extended and original account of the principle, decisively rejected the idea of Hobbes and Puffendorf that sovereignty could be transferred or delegated provided that it was done in a legitimate manner with the full consent of all concerned.

Rousseau's insistence on the indivisible aspect of sovereignty separates him from the liberal thinkers who had advocated its division and delegation as a means of protecting the people against tyranny; in their view, when sovereignty became absolute, it easily led to despotism. In France, Montesquieu, following what he believed to be the example of the English constitution, advocated the separation of the legislative, executive and judiciary bodies as a means of securing a proper balance of power in the State and preventing the degeneration of the monarchy.

Although Rousseau, in his concept of sovereignty, is closer to Hobbes than to the jurists, liberal thinkers or Montesquieu, he makes an important modification which brings him into line with the supporters of natural law: while sovereignty is absolute in the sense that it can be subjected to no constitutional limitation, there is an important sense in which it is limited by its own essential nature. Hobbes had agreed that sovereignty involved some obligation since the ruler's task was to provide for the safety of the people — and this included not mere self-preservation but 'all other contentments of life, which every man by lawful industry, without danger or hurt to the Commonwealth, shall acquire to himself' — but this tended to be a pragmatic and perhaps psychological principle. Whilst Locke did not dispute the importance of self-preservation and security, he was concerned primarily with the well-being of the individuals who make up the State rather than with the State as a separate entity. The thinkers of the

Natural Law School related sovereignty much more explicitly to the notion of the 'general good', treating it as power exercised for a rational purpose and as such compelled to pay heed to the demands of natural law.

While stressing its absolute quality, Rousseau devotes a whole chapter to the 'limits of sovereign power'. Sovereignty, though absolute, is not arbitrary, for it cannot go against the law of its own being. Since the function of 'all the common power' is the preservation and well-being of the whole community, it is inconceivable that it should be used for any other purpose. In this respect it is not dissimilar from the role of *amour de soi* in the individual — an 'absolute passion' and primordial need which develops from mere self-preservation to higher forms of 'interest' and self-realization. 'It is impossible that the body should wish to harm all its members.' 'By the sole fact that it is, the sovereign is always everything it should be.' It is not a physical power existing simply as such, but physical power directed towards a particular goal: the preservation of the community. It seems not unreasonable to conclude — although Rousseau himself does not do so — that sovereignty, like *amour de soi*, must be essentially 'good'. No doubt political life will be complicated and corrupted by other factors, as we shall see, but, as long as the State itself exists, these can never be allowed to destroy its ultimate basis.

As soon as sovereignty seeks to express itself — again like 'self-love' in the individual — it becomes inseparable from an act of will. The will that is here in question is not the ordinary will of a particular individual, but the will of the citizen as a member of the sovereign body. In other words, sovereignty is expressed as the 'general will' — a notion already briefly mentioned in the article on 'Political Economy'[2] . This notion, which is central to Rousseau's thought, has generated more discussion — and disagreement — than any other and it is perhaps rather strange that Rousseau himself never explicitly defined what he meant by the term. Yet when it is set within the context of his thought as a whole — and this involves not merely his political theory but his general philosophy of man — its meaning can be made fairly clear: the general will lifts the individual above selfish petty interests and enables him to identify himself with the common good, which is also his own higher good. It emerges from the social setting, but it expresses itself through a collective action based on a rational and moral principle. In this respect, the general will retains an integrity and firmness often lacking in the wayward reactions of the individual acting in response to his own emotions and passions. 'The general will is always constant, incorruptible and pure', and is always directed upon worthy objectives: 'peace, unity and equality'.

It is interesting to note that the expression 'general will' had already appeared in Diderot's *Encyclopaedia* article 'Natural Right', and the more limited political notion of will had been used earlier still by the jurists. Unlike Rousseau, however, Diderot sees the general will as an innate universal characteristic that can be a decisive factor in the establishment of social and political relations. Evidence for the existence of this general will is to be found, he asserts, in 'the laws of all civilized nations, the social actions of savage barbarous peoples, the tacit agreement made by mankind's enemies among themselves'. For Rousseau, on the other hand, the general will has no such universal significance since it does not appear until the organized social community has been established; it is not an innate human impulse but the expression of social morality.

In spite of its moral status as a force tending always towards 'the preservation and well-being of the whole' (as Rousseau puts it in his article 'Political Economy'), the general will does not always predominate in any particular society, for, like all other moral principles, it can be abused: its purity and constancy may not be strong enough to prevent its voice being stifled by the power of emotion, passion and prejudice. Men are not mere will, but complex human beings who often put self-interest before the general good. Even when they are acting as a body, the 'general will' may yield to the force of the 'will of all', for the citizens may weakly give way to the pressure of particular impulses concerned with their own selfish ends rather than with the common good. 'Each individual', says Rousseau, 'may as a man have a particular will contrary to or dissimilar from the general will he has as a citizen.' A truly virtuous man, like a truly virtuous citizen, needs to be able to resist personal emotion and passion, so that civil virtue, as he had already stated in his article, 'is only the conformity of the particular will to the general' (III, 252).

Yet even when the real nature of the general will is recognized, it still needs to be given an objective and stable form. In view of the possible inability of the will to sustain its momentum, it has to be related to a firm and clearly intelligible expression of its principal requirements. In other words, it must be embodied in 'the law', if it is to provide the effective basis of any legitimate society. Rousseau does not think that the definition of the law requires an abstruse metaphysical discussion about the 'laws of nature'; being created by man, the laws of society will obviously retain the characteristics of the human impulse inspiring them — in this case, the general will which is concerned with the well-being of the community. In the article 'Political Economy' Rousseau, as we have seen, had written about the law in lyrical terms, describing it as a 'celestial voice'. In the *Social Contract* he asserts that without the laws the State is 'like a body without a soul' (III, 248). The law, as the objective embodiment of the general will, is thus necessary for the moral well-being and the very survival of the community.

With the establishment of a law consistent with the requirements of sovereignty and general will Rousseau lays down the essentially democratic or, as he prefers to say, 'republican' basis of his conception of political society. 'So I call "republic" any State ruled by laws, whatever may be the form of administration, for then only public interest governs, and the *res publica* is a reality. All legitimate government is republican' (III, 379). In this respect it is true to say, as he does in the *Encyclopaedia* article, that, politically speaking, 'the voice of the people is the voice of God' (III, 246).

Unfortunately the achievement of this political ideal encounters a grave initial difficulty: how can men who, until they form part of an organized society, are little more than a 'blind multitude', carry out 'an enterprise as great and difficult as a system of legislation'? Men may indeed always will the good, but they do not always see it and behave in a rational way; they may have the will to achieve the good, but they do not necessarily have the judgement to do so. This means that they may be in need of some higher form of enlightenment. Here we see appearing on the horizon of Rousseau's thought a figure who seems at first sight to threaten its popular and democratic basis. Just as Emile had needed an almost omnipotent tutor and Saint-Preux, the hero of *La Nouvelle Héloïse*, an almost superhuman guide in the person of M. de Wolmar, so does this incipient society require an exceptional figure — the Lawgiver — to provide it with shape and substance. Rousseau tries to limit the authoritarian element by stressing that such a being has no legal power to impose his will; he has to persuade men through the force of his innate genius; he is a god-like figure who helps them to become true citizens. Moreover, the role of the Lawgiver is confined for the most part to the establishment of society; as soon as this has been achieved, the 'mechanic who invents the machine' leaves the citizens with the task of running it. Ultimate political responsibility will thus be handed over to the very people he has helped to create. In Rousseau's opinion, the Lawgiver is not imposing some alien unnatural power on the citizens but helping them to find the fulfilment of their higher nature and so make them fit to control their own destiny as free men.

In his discussion of the Lawgiver's role Rousseau is once again indulging in one of his favourite themes — rebirth. He is giving men a new being, and with it a new society. In *La Nouvelle Héloïse*, he had already spoken of 'beings recreated with a second nature'. The society for which the Lawgiver is responsible is a young and vigorous one, a virgin people unsullied by contemporary vice. Perhaps this dream of initiating a new society was what attracted Rousseau later on to the idea of drafting new constitutions for Poland and Corsica. It is interesting to note that he abandons all serious hope of reforming large nations, which he considers to be too far advanced in corruption for any remedy to be effective; his main concern is to try to check the onset of corruption in comparatively small and unsophisticated peoples like the Corsicans or (as he hoped at one stage) his own native Geneva.

The uncompromising nature of Rousseau's fundamental principles does not exclude a large degree of relativity and pragmatism when it comes to giving them specific application. In his political as in his religious views, there is a strongly conservative element which to some extent limits the radical implication of his main principles. He acknowledges that the 'force of things' is apt to counteract the 'force of legislation' and that powerful pressures will always threaten to divert the legislator and the citizens from their true goal. In his desire to escape from mere utopianism, Rousseau insisted that there was no universal blueprint valid for every country. On the other hand, he was equally convinced that the adoption of a particular constitution could never be an arbitrary choice: even though there was no universal ideal, there was a constitution ideally suited to the needs of each nation.

This point clearly emerges from his discussion of government. Rousseau's originality is to have made a clear and fundamental distinction between sovereignty and government, relegating the latter to a purely executive and subordinate role. Because sovereignty is the supreme legislative power, it will always be superior to the government which depends on it for its authority. Government has no absolute significance in itself and may assume may different forms. There are as many forms of governments as there are nations, but 'there must be one and only one government that is proper and good in a State at any one time'. The choice of a government suitable to a particular country has to reckon with various physical, psychological and historical factors such as climate, size of territory and population, national character and traditions. Following the example of predecessors such as Aristotle, Plato, Bodin, Hobbes and Montesquieu, Rousseau attempts a classification of different types of government, concluding that there are three main ones: democracy, aristocracy and monarchy. He points out that 'democracy' is quite different from modern 'representative' government and is closer to the view of the Ancients who identified it with direct government by the people. As he admits, a true democracy has probably never existed, for it would require the participation of all the citizens in the running of the State. In fact, democracy is valid only for a small community of men capable of exercising a superhuman control over their passions and interests. In practice, it is an unstable goverment, exposed to internal strife and discord. Monarchy too has serious drawbacks and the moderate tone of Rousseau's observations cannot conceal a deep mistrust. 'Kings want to be absolute', which means that they are always likely to put their own power above everything else. Moreover, the concentration of political authority in the hands of a single person is fraught with danger, for behind the monarch there always lurks the figure of the despot. For Rousseau the most satisfactory form of government is an aristocracy in its elective — and not its hereditary — form. 'It is the best and most natural order that the wisest govern the multitude, when one is sure that they will govern for its profit and not their own' (III, 166). Rousseau thinks that aristocracy is to be preferred because, being based on the principle of moderation, it offers a compromise between the extremes of democracy and monarchy; an artistocracy based on merit, as a properly elective aristocracy should be, gives the responsibility of government to those most suited to it by talent and position. Rousseau believes that, in general, monarchy, with all its drawbacks, is best suited to large states, democracy to very small, impoverished ones, and aristocracy to medium-sized, moderately prosperous ones. The true aim of any government, however, should always be the same: 'the preservation and prosperity of the members of the political association'.

The recognition that political theory must make some concessions to relativism, especially when it comes to applying general principles to particular situations, shows Rousseau's indebtedness to Montesquieu, even though the ultimate intention of the *Social Contract* and the *Spirit of the Laws* was quite different, the former claiming to deal with political right and the latter with existing governments. Rousseau admits that 'the general objects of every good institution must be modified in each country by the relations which originate in the local situation as well as in the characters of the inhabitants.' 'Apart from the maxims which are common to all, each people has some cause which applies them in a particular way and makes its legislation peculiarly its own' (III, 393). It is significant that Rousseau begins one of his chapters by quoting Montesquieu's dictum: 'freedom, not being a fruit of every climate, is not within the reach of every people'. Historical and geographical conditions demonstrate that 'every form of government is not suited to every country' (III, 414-6).

Like Rousseau, Montesquieu had stressed the importance of morality as an essential constituent of a healthy political society, but he had defined its influence in a rather different way. Whereas Rousseau believed morality to be indissolubly linked with politics as a pervasive and inescapable influence, Montesquieu had attributed a different kind of moral principle to each form of government: honour to monarchy, virtue to republic and fear (or the absence of morality) to despotism. In the *Social Contract* Rousseau takes issue with his predecessor on this point, criticizing him for having restricted virtue to republics: 'A famous author has made virtue the main principle of a republic, for all these conditions could not survive without virtue: but through having failed to make the necessary distinctions, this fine genius has often lacked accuracy and sometimes clarity, and has not seen that supreme authority being everywhere the same, the same principle must be found in every well-constituted State, to a greater or lesser degree, it is true, according to the form of government' (II, iv).

Another thinker who probably reminded Rousseau of the need to adapt absolute principles to the requirements of political reality was Machiavelli. Curiously enough, Rousseau does not see him as a supporter of unscrupulous opportunism but as a geniune patriot and republican who, though secretly hating despotism, was impelled to present his views in a satirical form. In this respect however, Rousseau was following an eighteenth-century tradition which owed a great deal to the view expressed by Spinoza in his *Tractatus politicus:* 'Machiavelli was a far-seeing man who was favourable to freedom'. In his *Historical and Critical Dictionary* Bayle had reservations about Machiavelli as a defender of freedom but readily granted that he had been animated by the 'republican spirit'. Diderot's article 'Machiavelli' in the *Encyclopaedia*, which appeared after the publication of the *Social Contract*, interpreted *The Prince* as a work intended to put people on their guard against the 'ferocious beast' of tyranny. Already in his article 'Political Economy' Rousseau had praised Machiavelli's 'satires' (i.e. *The Prince)* for attacking despotism. In the *Social Contract* he again praises Machiavelli: 'While pretending to give lessons to kings, he has given great lessons to nations. Machiavelli's *Prince* is the book for republicans' (III, vi). In a note he adds that Machiavelli was 'a gentleman and a good citizen' who had to conceal his love of liberty and

111

attachment to republican freedom. Rousseau's acceptance of the allegedly satirical aspect of Machiavelli's work may also have led him to ponder the problem of adapting ethical principles to the demands of political necessity. Like Machiavelli, Rousseau recognizes the powerful influence of human egoism and suggests that it is sometimes not prudent or desirable for the legislator to present the people with a direct statement of political truth. Historically, the 'fear of the gods' has often been a means of securing the people's obedience to sound human laws. Rousseau even quotes Machiavelli's principle that 'there has never existed a legislator who has not had recourse to the intermediary of a god to secure the acceptance of laws which would certainly not have been accepted in any other way'. Numa, insists Machiavelli, subdued a fierce people by using religion as 'the surest and most necessary support for civil society'. Although such methods are no longer applicable to modern man, Rousseau realizes that the demands of political reality may lead legislators to an attitude of pragmatism and compromise in the application of their essential principles.

In spite of the idealistic fervour animating the analysis of his fundamental principles, Rousseau recognizes that, in practice, governments cannot escape the pressure of an egoism that will affect most men, whether they are acting as individuals or as citizens. Every government, though deriving its authority from the sovereign people, has 'a particular ego' a sensibility common to its members, a force and a will of its own, tending to its own preservation' (III, i; III, 399). This means that it is exposed to the tensions and weaknesses belonging to any individual or collective body with well-defined physical and psychological characteristics. Collective bodies, therefore, tend to be as selfish as ordinary men; the very fact that the government consists of human beings with their usual passions and emotions constitutes a serious danger to the State and makes it imperative for the citizens to be on their guard against the abuse of this delegated power. In his correspondence with the Marquis de Mirabeau, Rousseau frankly admitted the gravity of the problem. 'How is it possible', he asks, 'to persuade men to obey the laws when it seems (superficially at least) in their interest to disobey them? This is a problem as difficult as the mathematical one of squaring the circle' (*CC*, XXXIII, 243). Although he was wont to praise ancient peoples for the moral vigour and resilience which enabled them to rise above human weakness (the last part of the *Social Contract,* for example, is devoted to a long account of Roman institutions and the way they could be adapted to meet unexpected crises), he acknowledges that modern man is too deeply corrupted to be able to imitate such illustrious predecessors.

Rousseau's desire to provide the citizens with a moral sanction that would strengthen their loyalty to the State through a willing obedience to the laws probably explains his decision to add a chapter on 'Civil Religion' to the *Social Contract.* At first sight this late addition may seem to be inconsistent with the predominantly secular emphasis of the rest of the work. Nevertheless, the idea of a 'civil religion' was one that Rousseau had held for some time; it is explicitly mentioned in the letter he wrote to Voltaire on Providence in 1756: 'I should like there to be in each state a moral code, a kind of civil profession of faith which would contain, positively, the social maxims which everyone would be obliged to acknowledge and, negatively, the intolerant maxims which he would be obliged to reject, not as impious but as seditious. Thus, any religion which could agree with the code would be allowed, any religion which did not agree with it would be proscribed, and everybody would be free to have none other than the code itself. This work, carefully prepared, would be, it seems to me, the most useful that has ever been composed, and perhaps the only one necessary to men' (IV, 1073-4).

It may also be significant that the first manuscript indications of this new chapter are to be found on the back of a page dealing with the figure of the Lawgiver, who is given a quasi-religious status. The introduction of the Lawgiver already suggests that Rousseau had doubts about men's ability to achieve political wisdom without the help of a superior being. The remarkable admission to the Marquis de Mirabeau about the impossibility of 'squaring the circle' of self-interest and obedience to the laws reveals a vein of pessimism in Rousseau's political thought. He was constantly returning to the problem of avoiding instability and internecine division in the State; he saw selfishness as a permanent threat to the achievement of the 'general good'. Elsewhere in the *Social Contract* Rousseau mentions man's need to possess god-like qualities if he is to find political fulfilment. Desirable though it may be as an ideal, democracy, he avers, is such a perfect government that it is not suitable for men: 'if there were a nation of gods, it would govern itself democratically'. Likewise, although it can be granted that 'all justice comes from God' as its sole source, the reality of human nature makes it necessary for men to have conventions and laws which they may be forced to obey. Nevertheless, the law itself, though a human invention, should retain something of its divine origin, which no doubt explains Rousseau's fervent praise of it, in the article on 'Political Economy', as a 'celestial voice that teaches man to imitate here below the immutable decrees of the divinity'.

The *Profession of Faith of the Savoyard Priest* had also dealt briefly with the problem of social unity and, in spite of the radical implications of a 'natural religion' valid for all men, Rousseau insisted that society might need a uniform public worship to protect the nation against internal strife and disunity. He accepted the principle of *cuius regio eius religio*, which meant that the ruler had the right to settle the form of public worship and even forbid the introduction of a new religion into the State. 'I regard all religions as so many salutary institutions which lay down in each country a uniform way of honouring God by public worship and which all have their reasons in climate, government, the genius of the people and in some other local cause, which may make one preferable to another, according to time and place. I believe them all to be good when they help people to serve God properly' (IV, 627).

In view of this it is not enough for each individual simply to accept the tenets of natural religion in his own heart. God no doubt is the ultimate source of order, but it is necessary for men to adapt themselves to this order and express it in such a way that their personal beliefs are related to their immediate social and political situation. The purpose of a 'civil religion', therefore, is to commit the citizen publicly to those aspects of natural religion which involve his participation in the community as a whole. Rousseau is careful to point out that it is not, strictly speaking, a question of religious dogmas but of 'feelings of sociability' aimed at inducing the citizens to 'love their duties'. In *Emile* he had already insisted that, when people forget religion, they also forget their human obligations. As he told a correspondent in 1764, 'take away eternal justice and the continuation of my being after this life and I see in virtue nothing but folly adorned with a fine name' (*CC*, XIX, 199). As far as possible Rousseau wants to dispense with the use of legal sanctions (he constantly affirms that the strength of a community lies in the hearts of the citizens rather than in any set of laws), but he admits that it may not be possible to avoid the need for a public acceptance of basic religious principles. 'These will be simple and few in number, precisely stated without explanations or commentaries; the existence of a powerful, intelligent and beneficent divinity, far-sighted and provident; the life to come; the happiness of the just; the punishment of the wicked; the sanctity of the social contract and the laws; these are the positive dogmas. As for the negative dogmas, I limit them to a single one — intolerance' (III, 468-9).

It would seem that Rousseau requires each citizen to accept the tenets of a 'civil religion' and, at the same time, the form of public worship laid down by the ruler. Yet as long as he does not openly oppose the national religion, he is free to follow his own conscience and beliefs; it is simply a matter of social discipline — *une affaire de police* — and there will be no question of forcing the individual to accept particular religious dogmas. What then becomes of Christianity in such a situation? At the outset of his discussion of civil religion, Rousseau makes it clear that Christianity in its perfect, ideal form does not provide a suitable basis for the citizens' religious life. In the first place, it is otherwordly; since it urges men to seek salvation in the next world, it is a 'spiritual religion concerned solely with heavenly matters; the Christian's fatherland is not of this world'. Even though he does his duty, the Christian is not deeply concerned with the well-being of the State and he is unlikely to do very much to promote the 'social spirit'. In merely human terms too the religion of the Gospel, 'sacred, sublime and true though it may be', teaches that all men are brothers and that 'the society which unites them is not abolished at death'. As such this religion does not generate the exclusive limited feelings needed to sustain genuine patriotism.

115

Rousseau mentions two contrasting views of Christianity: the first is the paradox of Pierre Bayle, according to which religion is of no use to the State since true Christians could not form a permanent political association. This idea had already been discussed by Montesquieu in the *Spirit of the Laws* (Book XXIV, chap. II) and it may be the reading of this chapter which prompted Rousseau's own comments. Montesquieu, however, rejected Bayle's suggestion and argued that true Christian principles could provide very effective help for the enlightened and conscientious discharge of civic duties. Secondly, Rousseau refers to William Warburton (1698-1779), the Bishop of Gloucester who, in *The Alliance of Church and State* (1736) and the *Divine Legation of Moses* (1737-41), had pressed for the introduction of Christian principles into political life. Rousseau's advocacy of a 'civil religion' means that he agreed with neither Bayle nor Warburton. The reference to intolerance as a 'negative' aspect of civil religion also shows him to be sympathetic to the criticism which so many *philosophes* directed against Christianity, especially in its Roman Catholic form, namely, that it led to intolerance and persecution. Rousseau thinks that the Church, by constantly seeking to impose its will on the citizens, will threaten the State with internal conflict. Indeed it would appear that Christianity, as a religion preaching 'servitude and dependence', is likely to support tyranny, for 'Christians are made to be slaves'. In any case, civil religion, being related directly to the social pact which in turn limits sovereignty to the principle of public good, will be concerned with the citizens' opinions only in so far as they affect the community. The sole opinions relevant to the State are those appertaining to morality and civic duties. 'Apart from that, everybody can have any opinions he wants, without the sovereign being in any way concerned with knowing about them, for as he has no competence in the other world, whatever may be the fate of the subjects in the life to come, it is not his business, provided they are good citizens in this life' (III, 468).

Rousseau draws from these ideas a conclusion that many critics have found very disturbing: anyone who does not accept the precepts of the civil religion will be banished from the State or even put to death. The thinker who has so vigorously opposed 'theological intolerance' declares: 'Let anyone who, after publicly recognizing these same dogmas, behaves as though he did not believe in them, be put to death; he has committed the greatest of crimes: he has lied before the law' (III, 468). The *Profession of Faith* had also stressed the need to safeguard social unity. 'Let us preserve public order; in every country let us respect the laws; let us not disturb the public worship prescribed by law; let us not lead the citizens to disobedience; for we certainly do not know whether it is a good thing for them to abandon their opinions for others, but we certainly know that it is a bad thing to disobey the laws.' In his *Letter* to the Archbishop of Paris, Rousseau had expressed himself still more emphatically, declaring that 'he who disobeys the laws disobeys God' (IV, 978).

The severe penalties which Rousseau would exact for the rejection of civil religion, though shocking to progressive liberal opinion, were not inconsistent with his own strongly moral view of political principles or with his almost obsessive concern with political and social harmony. Although a thinker like Bayle, who had put forward the idea of a society of virtuous atheists, seems today more progressive and enlightened than Rousseau, the latter's hostility to atheism and irreligion is also to be found in philosophers whose political outlook was much more liberal than his. To many it seemed that anyone who rejected the religious basis of social morality must be either a criminal or a madman and so ought to be forcibly restrained from doing harm to the State. Locke, for example, in his *Letter on Toleration* wrote: 'Those are not at all to be tolerated who deny the being of God. Promises, covenants and oaths, which are the bonds of human society, can have no hold upon an atheist. The taking away of God, though but even in thought, dissolves all' (first *Letter concerning Toleration*). An important representative of the School of Natural Law, Samuel Puffendorf, had given uncompromising support to the same idea, insisting that it was the State's duty to mete out 'the most rigorous punishment' to those who 'try to shake or destroy in any manner whatsoever, the accepted opinion of God's existence'. Plato, too, whom Rousseau greatly admired, had insisted in the tenth book of *The Laws* that atheism and impiety should be punished by imprisonment. Finally, Rousseau cannot have been unmindful of the attitude of his native Geneva towards the same problem: his fellow-citizens were still committed to Calvin's belief that religion was essential to civil life and that it was the State's duty to ensure that the relationship was securely maintained.

Through this insistence on the indissoluble bond between religion and politics Rousseau no doubt hoped to bridge the gap between the human and civil aspects of man's existence. He wanted the individual to live at peace in a harmonious and unified State, since without such an environment it would be impossible for him to find personal happiness and fulfilment. As we have seen, Rousseau is constantly reproaching modern life for the way in which it puts man in contradiction with himself. His constructive philosophy had constantly striven to overcome that fatal inner division by developing a unified view of human existence. Yet he realised that, however successful might be the individual's effort to achieve personal self-realisation, this could not be made stable or permanent if he lived in an environment that threatened his inner peace by confronting him with the possibility of continual strife. This is why Rousseau did not hesitate to put forward ideas which, though consistent with his own aim, seemed to be at variance with those of the progressive thinkers of his time.

6. Practical Politics

The presence of a Genevan element in Rousseau's political thought has to be related to the fact that Geneva was the only authority to condemn the *Social Contract* during the author's lifetime. This condemnation, however, owed as much to the work's repercussions upon the Genevan political situation as to any serious analysis and appraisal of its philosophical principles. In spite of the fulsome praise often bestowed by Rousseau upon his native republic, many leading Genevans had serious misgivings about the ultimate effect of his ideas upon their political life, largely because of the discrepancy between fact and theory. Although some of Rousseau's ideas were to be found in the original Genevan constitution — for example, the sovereignty of the people, the equality of citizens' rights, the need for periodic assemblies — they had no place in actual practice. Far from being a democracy, Geneva was almost an oligarchy: power remained in the hands of a few rich and influential families who provided members for the two Councils — the Council of Two Hundred and the Council of Twenty-Five — which virtually controlled the republic. By stressing a principle like the absolute sovereignty of the people, Rousseau's treatise could make the Genevans aware that their existing political authority was to a large extent based on usurpation.

The political inequality existing in the republic is borne out by the social and legal groups into which the population was divided.[1] There were first of all the 'citizens' and the *bourgeois*. A 'citizen' (a title which Rousseau proudly claimed for himself) had to be the son of a citizen and born in Geneva, while a *bourgeois*, though not a citizen, had bought *lettres de bourgeoisie* which gave him a vote but debarred him from the magistrature; the 'natives' were people born in Geneva but denied the status of citizens, while 'inhabitants' or foreigners were those who had bought the right to live in Geneva and were forced to pay heavier taxes than the citizens; 'subjects' included mercenary soldiers, peasants coming from outlying regions, beggars and others who had no effective political position. At one stage in the eighteenth century, all classes united to oppose the aristocracy controlling the little Council; this was not due simply to resentment at an alleged usurpation of power but also to a dislike of the French manners and morals which, it was maintained, were being introduced into Geneva by this patrician group; the poorer members of the community held fast to the republican tradition and remained loyal to ancient values. A sense of social injustice, combined with a strong element of patriotism, helped to draw together the lower social groups in their opposition to the powerful oligarchy. As the son of an artisan (his father was a clock-maker), Jean-Jacques, though a 'citizen', had a fairly lowly social status and, as Michel Launay points out,[2] he seems to have identified himself from his earliest years with the opponents of the ruling faction. At the same time his departure from Geneva at the age of sixteen prevented him from being directly involved in Geneva's political affairs and his view of his native republic often owed as much to personal ideas and feelings as to an objective appraisal of the real situation.

Those Genevans who felt themselves to have been dis-possessed of their proper rights sometimes managed to enlist Rousseau's support and ultimately succeeded in engaging him in controversy with the authorities (especially after the con-demnation of the *Social Contract* in 1762), the result being the polemical *Lettres Écrites de la Montagne (Letters Written from the Mountain)* of 1764, which sought to refute the charges levelled against him by the *procureur-général*, Jean-Robert Tronchin, in his *Letters Written from the Country* (1763).[3] Of more immediate interest, however, are the broader philo-sophical and political implications of Rousseau's comments on the Genevan way of life. It has already been pointed out that the *Discourse on the Arts and Sciences* was in some respects a reaffirmation of the simplicity of ancient moral values against the corruption of contemporary life, so that Geneva and the Swiss cantons could be seen as examples of an older moral tradition that was still surviving in the modern world. He again identified himself with Geneva when in 1754 he decided to dedicate the *Discourse on the Origin of Inequality* to the Republic; shortly after making this dedication he was re-admitted to the Church of Geneva and given back his citizen's rights.

The *Dédicace* offers Rousseau's fellow-citizens a view of their republic that anticipates in some respects the ideal society depicted in the *Social Contract*. At the very outset, for example, he insists that Geneva is an admirable example of a state that has remained close to natural law while being 'favourable to society, the maintenance of public order and the happiness of individuals'. As well as being small enough for the citizens to have the advantage of 'seeing and knowing one another' in a way that encourages a genuine feeling of patriotism, Geneva is a 'democratic and wisely tempered' republic in which 'people and sovereign are the same person' (III, 112). Genevans 'live and die free' because 'nobody is above the law' and no-one outside the State can impose any alien law upon it. The 'right of legislation' is common to all the citizens, for 'who can know better than they under what conditions they agree to live together in the same society?'

Rousseau's emphasis on the unity of Geneva and the apparent equality of its citizens was likely to displease the rulers of the Republic, because it was an uncomfortable reminder that they were usurping power that properly be-longed to all the citizens. At the same time, Rousseau was reinforcing the resentment of those humbler members of the Republic who were becoming increasingly conscious of their exclusion from political authority. Since Rousseau's sym-pathies lay with the underprivileged, his dream of a new, regenerated Geneva would inevitably arouse the hostility of an oligarchy only too anxious to maintain the *status quo*. Never-theless, he persisted in his efforts to see Geneva as a symbol of his political ideal, for at the very beginning of the *Social Contract* he reminded his readers of his own political origins. 'As I was born the citizen of a free State and a member of the sovereign body, the right to vote on public affairs is enough to impose on me the duty of instructing myself in them, however feeble my voice may be. Whenever I reflect on governments, I am happy to find always in my investigations new reasons for loving the government of my country' (III, 351).

ın spıte oı Rousseau's continued affection for his native republic, it would be misleading to see his political ideas in exclusively Genevan terms. Precisely because his ideas were related to an idealised — and not the real — Geneva, they could be modified by other traditions. Already as a child he had been subjected to the powerful influence of Antiquity. In a well-known passage in the *Confessions* he relates how 'Plutarch became his favourite reading': 'From these interesting readings and the conversations to which they gave rise between my father and me, there was formed the free republican spirit, the indomitable and proud character, impatient of yoke and servitude which has tormented me during my whole life in situations least suitable for giving it expression. Constantly occupied with Rome and Athens, living so to speak with their great men, born myself the citizen of a republic and the son of a father whose love of his country was his greatest passion, I was fired by his example; I believed myself to be a Greek or Roman; I would become the character whose life I was reading' (I, 9). In his later career it was not unusual for him to associate ancient Rome with Geneva. Claire, one of the characters in *La Nouvelle Héloïse*, says that 'if she had been born in Geneva, she would have had a completely Roman soul' (II, 657). The strongly patriotic and Genevan tone of the *Letter to d'Alembert* did not prevent Rousseau from constantly referring to the great merits of Antiquity: Greek tragedy, as we have had occasion to note, was contrasted with the decadence of the modern theatre while, in a more general way, the Ancients' attitude towards entertainment showed a greater respect for moral values than the 'reversal of natural relationships characteristic of present-day life. In the *Social Contract* the influence of Rome is more directly discernible than that of Geneva, for most of the fourth book is taken up with an analysis of Roman institutions: there Rousseau tries to show how the Romans protected political stability by adapting their institutions to unexpected crises; the history of Rome proves that a State cannot survive by merely adapting or inventing political machinery but only by constantly reaffirming the citizens' moral integrity and sense of personal responsibility. At other times too Rousseau will quote Sparta as a remarkable example of civic pride: it was a state which, as he put it in the

Letter to d'Alembert, 'he will never have quoted enough for the example we ought to draw from it'. The civic sense of the Ancients offered a remarkable contrast to the modern spirit which despised patriotism and religion. Rousseau delighted in invoking 'these venerable images of antiquity where I can see men raised by sublime institutions to the highest degree of greatness and virtue attainable by human wisdom' (II, 538, 1536).

An analysis of the formative influences on Rousseau's political ideas has to recognize the importance of distinguishing between their universal and particular aspects. Rousseau himself said of the *Social Contract*: 'In this work I have not gone beyond general considerations. I have not overstepped — nor could I overstep — the limits of a purely philosophical and political discussion' (*CC*, X, 122, 307). The point is also stressed in the *Confessions* when he describes his treatise as 'an enterprise in which I wished to use only the force of reasoning, without any trace of ill-humour or partiality' (I, 405 note). Few would dispute that the main concepts such as sovereignty, the law and general will are analysed in a highly abstract, almost mathematical manner. Rousseau's occasional introduction of a more emotional and imaginative note (for example, in his discussion of the Lawgiver) does not affect the intellectual emphasis of the work as a whole. In this respect it is probably useful to distinguish between the general, universally valid principles of political right (as Rousseau interprets them) and their application to particular cases. Rousseau's argument readily lends itself to this distinction in view of his decisive emphasis on the difference between sovereignty and government. As delegated responsibility, government may assume various forms, each of which can be explained and perhaps justified by a consideration of its historical, physical and psychological origins. Although there may be one particular government which suits each country, there can be no universal blueprint valid for all. This helps to explain Rousseau's claim that 'he had laboured for his fatherland and for little States constituted like it', and yet that, at the same time, his essential principles were valid for all States. 'If his doctrine could be of some use to others, it was by changing the objects of their esteem and perhaps thus delaying the decadence which they accelerate by their false judgements' (I, 935).

Interesting indications of Rousseau's attempt to balance the universal and relativist elements in his political thought are to be found in the two constitutions he prepared for Corsica and Poland. The Corsicans' rebellion against the republic of Genoa which had ruled them tyrannically for many years aroused a great deal of comment in the eighteenth century. It will be recalled that James Boswell produced *An Account of Corsica* in 1769 after a brief stay on the island in 1765. The Corsican leader and patriot Pasquale Paoli had been impressed by Rousseau's remark in the *Social Contract*: 'There is in Europe one State capable of legislation: it is the island of Corsica. The valour and persistence with which this brave people has known how to recover and defend its freedom well deserve that some man should teach it how to preserve that freedom. I have a presentiment that one day this little island will astonish Europe' (II, x). In 1764 another influential Corsican, Captain Mathieu Buttafoco, wrote to Rousseau about this same eulogy and expressed the hope that Jean-Jacques would be 'this wise man who could find the means of preserving this freedom which has cost so much blood' (*CC*, XXI, 85-8; 31 August 1764). In response to an invitation to draw up a constitution for the island, Rousseau eventually prepared a *Projet de Constitution pour la Corse*; it never got beyond the draft stage, for it was nullified by the French annexation of the island in 1769. For a time Rousseau hoped to visit Corsica, but finally refrained from doing so because of the difficult political situation. Even in its present form, however, the *Projet* is a revealing example of his attempts to apply the principles of the *Social Contract* to a particular nation.[4] That he intends to take the task quite seriously is shown by his request for precise details about the island and its inhabitants: he asked Buttafoco to send him 'an exact description of the island, its natural history, productions, culture, divisions and districts': all this, together with information about the size of the population, would enable him to know the Corsicans' 'natural genius'. As he also wrote to another correspondent, 'when it is a question of forming a body of people, it is necessary to know men and take them as they are' (*CC*, XXII, 229). The last phrase is the same as the one used in the introduction to the *Social Contract* when Rousseau spoke of 'taking men as they are and the laws as they can be'.

This project is all the more interesting because it is not only related to the general principles underlying Rousseau's political theory but it also contains several indications of the way in which his ideas were influenced by personal preferences and feelings, as well as by the more objective factors already mentioned. Corsica was a particularly appropriate subject for the realisation of his political ideal because towards the end of his life he spoke of living on an island; his personal and social aspirations, as critics have already pointed out, always had a very strongly 'insular' character, showing a marked preference for the small, circumscribed and largely self-sufficient community whose members enjoyed an open and happy relationship with one another. The picture of a regenerated Geneva in the *Letter to d'Alembert* and the description of the rural community of Clarens in *La Nouvelle Héloïse* already present the main elements of Rousseau's ideal community. The island of Corsica seemed to offer an excellent opportunity of applying these principles to a real situation.

At the outset Rousseau insists that it is much more important to shape the nation and develop its individual character than to decide on the precise form of government. No government, however skilfully devised it may be, can survive unless the nation it serves is healthy and strong. It is essential, therefore, for the Corsicans to be as self-sufficient and self-reliant as possible and to draw their maxims from their own experience. This is an essential condition of freedom, for 'whoever depends on others and does not have his resources in himself cannot be free' (III, 903). It is not a question of the Corsicans striving 'to become other than what they are but of knowing how to keep themselves as they are'. A nation's survival rests ultimately on the strength of its population and not on material goods. 'A State rich in money is always weak and a State rich in men is always strong' (III, 904).

To be vigorous, a population has to be active and, as far as the Corsicans are concerned, this means that they should direct their energies towards rural activities, developing to the utmost the agricultural resources of the island. Agriculture has the great advantage of making men contented with their lot and attaching them to the land of their birth. 'The only means of keeping a State in independence is agriculture.' Admittedly, commerce may seem to have the advantage of producing more money, but agriculture has the still greater advantage of ensuring freedom. Moreover, Rousseau constantly returns to another point: an agrarian community will enjoy the benefit of both simplicity and strength. In this respect its members will be very different from the effeminate and corrupt city-dwellers who spend their time and energy on unproductive occupations. Rural life, on the other hand, by keeping the inhabitants close to the land, will strengthen their attachment to their country and make them more patriotic. In this respect, too, an agrarian community will benefit from a wider and more even distribution of the population, whereas large towns, and especially capitals, exude a 'continual pestilence which undermines and destroys the nation'. Furthermore, it is important to ensure that there is genuine equality in the State and this can be achieved more easily with a hard-working population engaged in agriculture rather than in commerce.

The strength, simplicity and equality which characterise a 'rural system' require a democratic form of government. In support of this Rousseau invokes the example of Switzerland which is, in general, a 'poor and barren country' with a republican form of government. On the other hand, an aristocratic government is to be found in the more fertile and prosperous Swiss cantons. Although Corsica is a fertile island with a warmer climate than Switzerland, this does not affect the need for it to concentrate on the cultivation of the land. Even here no doubt a strictly democratic government involving the active participation of all the inhabitants is not possible, for such a government is more suited to a small town than to a whole nation. Since it is not feasible to make the whole population assemble in one place (as a true democracy would require), some degree of aristocratic government must be introduced and some absolute authority will have to be entrusted to delegates. Rousseau tries to overcome the difficulty by suggesting that Corsica should have a 'mixed government', which would require partial assemblies and fairly frequent changes of officials. In this way administration would be confined to a few people who could be carefully selected for their wisdom and intelligence; the population would also be able to spread over the whole island and yet feel that it was participating in the running of the country on equal terms. The result would be a balanced, well-distributed community, responsible and yet free.

The economic principle governing Corsican life is quite clear: 'Everybody must live but nobody must get rich' (III, 924). This means the exclusion of large-scale finance and restrictions on the use of money. To ensure this Rousseau suggests that the inhabitants should satisfy their material requirements by using the method of exchange. In a characteristically revealing expression Rousseau insists on the idea of exchange 'without intermediaries'. (In his own life he had always felt that money inhibited independence and the enjoyment of personal relations). In any case, commerce will be inimical to agriculture. Since the Corsicans will be largely self-sufficient, they will not need to engage in much foreign trade. Rousseau also reminds them that as 'finance' is a modern invention, they can usefully consider the old Roman idea of the 'public domain', which often meant that revenue took the form of goods rather than of money; magistrates and soldiers, for example, were paid in kind. Rousseau thinks it would be a good idea for the Corsicans to introduce the idea of *la corvée* or compulsory labour. He admits that this notion is an 'abomination' in France, where it is bitterly resented by the peasants who have to help with public work such as road-building instead of devoting themselves to their agricultural activities; in Switzerland, on the contrary, few people complain of such work.

Although Corsican society will be based on equality, it will not be completely egalitarian and Roussea suggests the division of society into three classes: 'citizens', 'patriots' and 'aspirants'. There would be no hereditary aristocracy, for social differences would depend on 'merit, virtue and service'. To become a 'citizen' a person would be required to take a solemn oath of loyalty to the nation and he would have to be more than twenty years old; in the course of time young 'aspirants' would qualify for entry into the other two classes. A 'patriot' would be a legally married 'aspirant' holding some property in his own right, while 'patriots' could become 'citizens' when they had two living children, their own home and enough land to ensure subsistence. Rousseau suggests that *corvées* should be given mainly to the young 'aspirants'; but citizens and patriots must take them to work and set them an example. 'Let all that is done for the public good be honourable. Let the magistrate himself, busy with other cares, show that this work is not beneath him, like those Roman consuls who, in order to set their troops an example, were the first to put their hand to the labours of the camp!' (III, 932-3).

The final effect of these various activities will be to strengthen the Corsicans' attachment to their country and to inspire them with a true sense of pride. How different is such pride, which involves the whole nation and is prompted by natural feelings and 'fine and great objects', from the vanity which is related to a selfish preoccupation with petty aims! 'As there is nothing more truly beautiful than independence and power, any nation which is being formed is first of all proud. But never was a young nation vain, for vanity is by its very nature individual; it can never be the instrument of such a great thing as the formation of a nation' (III, 938). The example of Switzerland and ancient Rome, to which Rousseau also calls attention in his *Projet*, is intended to strengthen the close bond uniting all Corsicans in their pursuit of a common aim, which is the well-being of their country and the happy freedom of its inhabitants.

In 1770 Rousseau was given another opportunity of applying his ideas to a real political situation, for he was invited by Count Wielhorski, acting on behalf of the Confederation of Bar, to make suggestions for the reform of the Polish constitution. The *Considérations sur le Gouvernement de Pologne et sur sa Réformation Projetée* is much more detailed and substantial than the Corsican project, even though it was a question of reforming an existing constitution and not of creating a new one. Once again, however, historical events — on this occasion the Partition of Poland in 1772 — prevented any effective use being made of Rousseau's work. The abbé Mably had been invited to undertake a similar task, and produced *Du Gouvernement et des Lois de la Pologne* (or the *Observations sur le Gouvernement de Pologne* as it is called in the original manuscript) which was published in the eight volume of his complete works in 1789. Rousseau and Mably were able to see each other's drafts while they were working on them and in a number of places it is obvious that Rousseau was commenting on the *philosophe*'s observations; this is all the more interesting when it is recalled that Mably was strongly republican and egalitarian in his ideas, usually appearing in the history of ideas as a predecessor — albeit an utopian one — of communism.[5]

Although the purpose of the present study does not allow for a detailed analysis of the *Considérations*, it will be worthwhile to indicate some of their main points since they have a bearing upon the earlier *Projet*, as well as upon the ideas of the *Social Contract* to which Rousseau often refers in the course of his observations. As in these earlier works, he is at pains to emphasise his oft-repeated point that political institutions, however carefully and ingeniously devised they may be, cannot survive unless the principles sustaining them are kept alive in the hearts of the citizens. He constantly urges the Poles to make freedom and patriotism live in their hearts. He repeats the point previously made in a letter to the Marquis de Mirabeau: to set the laws above man is as difficult as the mathematical problem of 'squaring the circle'. There will never be any good and sound constitution but the one in which the law reigns over the citizens' hearts' (III, 955). The principal task is 'so to establish the republic in the Poles' hearts that it will subsist in spite of all the efforts of its oppressors. That, it seems to me, is the only refuge which force can neither reach nor destroy' (III, 959).

The need to rely on inner strength rather than on formal laws and constitutions prompts Rousseau to denounce once again the corruption of modern society which has 'many law-makers but no legislator'. We are the victim of 'our prejudices, our base philosophy and the passions of petty interest selfishly concentrated in every heart by inept institutions which were never dictated by genius' (III, 956). This is yet another reason for turning towards the Ancients, for when we read their history we are 'transported into another universe and among other beings'. 'What have the French, English and Russians in common with the Romans and Greeks? Almost nothing except their faces. The strong souls of the latter seem to others like historical exaggerations' (ibid). From among the Ancients Rousseau singles out (as he does elsewhere) three great figures: Moses, Lycurgus and Numa. Moses achieved the astonishing feat of creating a nation and a free people out of 'a swarm of wretched refugees who were without arts, arms, talents, virtues and courage', and such was his achievement that the nation he formed still survives; Lycurgus undertook to establish a people already degraded by slavery and its concomitant vices and was so successful that Sparta became renowned for its fervent patriotism, giving laws to the whole of Greece and even striking fear in the Persian empire; Numa, far from being a mere inventor of rites and ceremonies, was 'the true founder of Rome, making it solid and durable by uniting brigands into an indissoluble body of citizens'. Compared with such legislators and those whom they served modern nations contain nothing but nonentities. 'A Frenchman, Englishman, Spaniard, Italian and Russian are almost all the same man'. The Poles, on the other hand, by following the example of the Ancients, can learn to become themselves. 'At twenty years of age a Pole must not be another man: he must be a Pole' (III, 966).

It is interesting to note that in this work — one of his last — Rousseau returns to a point so insistently made in the very first *Discourse*: that modern man is weak and enslaved, whereas the Ancients were remarkable for their 'vigour of soul'. The Poles' first task should be to attain a genuine inner strength which will enable them to resist the insidious corruption of the modern world. Without the moral force of 'virtue' (another word frequently used in the first *Discourse*) they will surely never resist the powerful and ruthless neighbours so eager to enslave them. This moral energy and effort of will, so necessary to keep their nation alive, must be related to a deep-seated patriotism; virtuous citizens will know how to make their own personal interests subservient to the needs of the nation and the public good.

In spite of its supreme importance in the national life, virtue alone — and even patriotism as a form of virtuous zeal — will not be enough to protect the new State against external danger. Here again, Rousseau drives home a point already made in the work on Corsica: the need of every nation to have a genuine

individuality and personality of its own. In this respect
Rousseau is realistic enough to recognize the importance of
psychological factors in the life of the most virtuous citizens.
Inner conviction and loyalty cannot be obtained by the use of
mere reason and morality; due account must also be taken of
senses and feelings. This is a point he makes at the very
beginning of the *Considérations*: it is essential for the Poles to
form acceptable and effective habits which may sometimes run
counter to the demands of reason. This means the abolition or
exclusion of all occupations which weaken the citizens' will.
On the other hand, games and entertainments of an active kind
are to be encouraged. Needless to say, the 'many public games
which the good motherland likes to see her children playing'
will not include the theatre, and Rousseau takes up the point so
energetically made in the *Letter to d'Alembert*: the theatre is a
restricting and unnatural entertainment which separates men
from one another; it is thus necessary to oppose 'all that makes
men effeminate, all that distracts and isolates them, makes
them forget their country and their duty ... They must invent
games, festivals, celebrations which are so suited to this Court
that they are not found in any other.' People must 'enjoy
themselves in Poland more than in other countries, but not in
the same way' (III, 963).

Since the nation must develop its own characteristics and
individuality (and Rousseau had insisted on the same point in
the case of the Corsicans), the citizen's whole personality —
and not just its rational and moral aspects — must be imbued
with patriotic feeling. In Rousseau's view, national institutions
are important because it is to them that the Poles' principles
and feelings can be attached. Virtuous and patriotic citizens
need such institutions to give 'a particular form' to their
'souls'. 'It is national institutions which form the genius,
character, tastes, morals and manners of a people, which cause
it to be itself and not another, which inspire this ardent love of
the fatherland based on habits that cannot be uprooted,
which make it die of boredom with other peoples in the midst
of delights of which it is deprived in its own' (III, 960). The
result of all this will be 'to give to their souls national features
which will distinguish them from other people ... They will
obey the laws and will not elude them, because these laws will

131

be suited to them and will have the inner assent of their will' (III, 961).

All this means that education will be given priority in the reformed Polish republic. 'It is education which must give souls national strength and so direct their opinions and tastes that they will be patriots by inclination, passion and necessity' (III, 966). This is all the more urgent as 'national education belongs only to free men; it is only they who have a common existence and are truly bound by the law'. Unlike Europeans who are born for enslavement, the Poles are destined for freedom. It is thus necessary for them to become steeped in their national heritage, which means being brought up with a thorough knowledge of the geography and history of their country. For the most part public education will prevail, although Rousseau does not exclude all private forms. Nevertheless, privately educated children will not be allowed to live apart from the rest but will be required to participate in public activities. Far from limiting themselves to their own personal pleasures, young Poles must play together in public, so that there is always 'a common aim to which they all aspire and which stimulates competition and emulation'; although their formal education may sometimes be 'domestic and private', 'their games must be public and common to all'. In other words, the entertainments appropriate to a reformed Poland will not be unlike those previously advocated by Rousseau for a regenerated Geneva. In both republics, 'equality, fraternity and competition will prevail', because the young will 'live before the eyes of the citizens and desire public approbation',

Once again Rousseau invokes the example of the Ancients. It will be necessary to follow 'roads unknown to the moderns and by which the Ancients led men to this vigour of soul, this patriotic zeal, this esteem for truly personal qualities, without any concern for what is alien to man'. In this respect Rousseau alludes to the principle which had inspired *Emile*. He reminds his readers that early education must be 'negative' because it is concerned primarily with the prevention of vice. The Poles can look confidently to the future because, in spite of all the obstacles facing them, they can trust in man's natural goodness or, as Rousseau puts it, there is 'in the hearts of all men a leaven which, in order to be fermented, is merely waiting to be animated by suitable institutions'. Poland can look forward to a 'second birth' which will make it 'happy and free' and give it 'all the vigour of soul of a new-born nation' (III, 970).

There is, however, a physical difficulty that has to be overcome; unlike Corsica, Poland is a comparatively large State, whereas true happiness and prosperity characterise small States, whatever their particular form of government. Extensive territory is the 'first and principal source of humanity's misfortunes'. 'Almost all small States, whether republican or monarchist, prosper by the mere fact that they are small; that all the citizens know and look at one another; that the rulers can see for themselves the harm which is being done and the good which has to be done; and that their orders are carried out before their very eyes.' All large nations, on the other hand, are 'crushed by their own mass'. 'It is only God who can govern the world and superhuman qualities would be required to govern large nations.' It is, therefore, essential for Poland to restrict its size by shedding any unnecessary territory and, as far as possible, adopting a federal system of government, this being 'the only one suited to both large and small States and the only one suited to Poland' (III, 971). Instead of being a large State, Poland should be a federation of small ones. 'If Poland were, as I should like it to be, a confederation of thirty-three little States, it would unite the strength of large monarchies and the freedom of small republics; but, for that, it would be necessary to give up ostentation, and I am afraid that is the most difficult point' (III, 1010).

As soon as he deals with constitutional details, Rousseau remains faithful to the main principles of the *Social Contract*, while recognizing the need to adapt them to this particular nation. From the very first he insists on the supremacy of the legislative power. 'As soon as the legislative power speaks, everything becomes equal again; all other authority is silenced by it; its voice is the voice of God on earth' (III, 973). It will be recalled that a similar expression has already been used in the article on 'Political Economy' [6] when Rousseau said that 'the voice of the people is the voice of God' (III, 247). The point is now vigorously re-affirmed. 'The law of nature, this sacred, indefeasible law which speaks to man's heart and reason, does not allow the legislative authority to be restricted.' At the same time no section of the community can be excluded from it because acceptance of the law requires personal assent.

As we know, the exalted position of the law is a necessary condition of freedom, but since freedom is not a mere abstraction, it can assume various forms. Already in the *Social Contract* Rousseau had called attention to Montesquieu's dictum that 'freedom, not being a product of all climates, is not within the grasp of all nations' and he reaffirms the point here : 'Freedom is a good food but requires a strong digestion ; you need very sound stomachs to stand it.' (He had used similar phraseology when he had discussed the Genevans' situation in the *Dedication* to the second *Discourse* : 'It is with freedom, as with these solid, succulent foods or these generous wines, suitable for nourishing and fortifying the robust temperaments which are used to them, but which overwhelm, ruin and intoxicate the weak and delicate ones which are not made for them' (III, 112-3). Freedom, therefore, involves personal effort and self-control. 'I laugh at these degraded peoples who, allowing themselves to be stirred up by trouble-makers, dare to speak of freedom without having any idea of it, and, with their hearts full of all the vices of slaves, imagine that in order to be free, it is enough to be disobedient. Proud and sacred freedom ! if these poor folk could know you, if they understood at what cost you are acquired and preserved, if they realised how much harder and more austere are your laws than the tyrants' yoke, their weak souls, enslaved by passions that ought to be stifled, would fear you a hundred times more than servitude ; they would flee from you in terror as though from a load that was about to crush them' (III, 974).

An example of the particular problem involved in bringing freedom to those who are not yet ready for it is provided by the liberation of the Polish serfs. Commendable though this step is in itself, it must be taken with great caution ; the serfs cannot be freed until they have been made worthy of freedom. In any case, the basic human aspects of the problem must never be overlooked. 'They are men like you ; in them they have the wherewithal to become like you.' It would be unwise, therefore, to free their bodies without first of all freeing their souls.

When he reaches the point of deciding on detailed methods of legislation, Rousseau is careful to stress a maxim repeatedly stated in other political writings — that it is extremely dangerous to have too many laws. As he had said in 'Political Economy', 'the more you multiply the laws, the more you make them despised' (III, 253). 'The most vicious of all peoples', he had affirmed in a fragment dealing with the same problem, 'is the one with most laws' (III, 493). As the *Social Contract* had constantly emphasised, one of the greatest dangers threatening any State is a political structure so complicated that the executive authority is always tempted to encroach on the legislative. The position of Poland is no exception : it is vital to protect the legislature from usurpation by the executive. He also recalls the principle established in the *Social Contract* : 'Any body entrusted with executive power tends firmly and continually to subjugate the legislative power and succeeds in doing so sooner or later' (III, 977, cf, III, 434-6). There are two ways of obviating this dangerous development. The first is not to let the government exist for too long. In Rousseau's opinion, the great defect of the English Parliament was its failure to do this. His second proposal is to divide the executive functions in a way that prevents them from uniting to oppress the legislative. If at the same time there are frequent changes of officials, this will prevent any sustained attempt at usurpation. Rousseau insists that those who exercise executive authority tend to become 'little despots who, without exactly usurping the sovereign authority, none the less oppress the citizens in detailed matters'. It is necessary to exercise constant vigilance because the distribution of executive power among several bodies will not entirely overcome the possibility of usurpation ; one particular body will always emerge as the most powerful and most likely to dominate the rest. Again Rousseau reminds us that the Ancients never used this device of creating separate chambers or departments to forestall usurpation. The Roman Senate, for example, while governing half the known world, never divided its authority (its members were also appointed for life) and yet it never usurped the legislative power.

Rousseau repeats another point emphatically made in the *Social Contract*: the dangers of representative government. Representation may be unavoidable in a large State, but, in Rousseau's eyes, it is a highly undesirable practice. 'At the very moment', he had stated in his earlier treatise, 'a people gives itself representatives, it is no longer free; it no longer exists' (III, 431). The legislator may be deceived, but never corrupted, whereas the exact opposite is the case with representatives, for they are deceived with difficulty but easily corrupted. He refers to the case of the English Parliament, and to the notorious *liberum veto* in Poland itself. 'A man who is mistaken can be enlightened, but how is it possible to hold back a man who sells himself?' (III, 979). Once again the only remedy is for the citizens to be eternally watchful and to ensure that the executive is doing everything under their critical gaze.

Since Poland is a large State, Rousseau concedes that it may have to be ruled by a monarch, which allows the possibility of usurpation. Even so, there may be no effective alternative to a king. Unlike Mably who suggested that such a king should have a merely decorative and symbolic role, Rousseau favours giving him real power. He believes that as soon as a king is made to realise that he cannot be a usurper, he will govern quite well and become the 'first citizen of the State'. Since kings are 'born judges of their peoples', it is quite appropriate for them to appoint their own representatives when they them-selves are unable to discharge some particular function. While decisively rejecting any idea of a hereditary monarchy, Rous-seau suggests that the king should be elected for life.

Of the three sources of possible anarchy in Poland — the *liberum veto*, the Confederation, and the existence of private armies — Rousseau categorically condemns only the last. In spite of the terrible abuses to which it has given rise, the *liberum veto* 'is not vicious in itself' since it was originally intended to protect national freedom; this 'wretched right' has unfor-tunately been transformed into an instrument of oppression through misuse. Rousseau suggests that it should be restricted to matters involving fundamental laws or general issues and that no single individual should be allowed to halt the State's business through the irresponsible use of the veto. It would be quite proper to punish such behaviour very severely, even by death. The Confederation could likewise be used to protect freedom and in its true 'federative form' it could become a 'political masterpiece'.

Whatever the particular area that is being reformed, Rous-seau insists that it is unwise to introduce unnecessary admin-

istrative and legal complications into the political body. Yet
again he appeals to the example of the Ancients who did
everything from a sense of duty and were never confined to
some specific function. 'By trade the citizens were neither
soldiers nor judges nor priests; they were everything through
duty. That is the true secret of making everything move
towards the common goal, of preventing the political spirit
from being identified with bodies at the expense of patriotism,
and the hydra of chicanery from devouring a nation' (III, 1000).
Justice, for example, needs only a 'few clear, simple laws'
capable of being interpreted by a few judges who can, if
necessary, rely on 'the natural enlightenment of rectitude and
good sense'. As in the *Social Contract*, Rousseau calls
attention to the traditional practice of dividing the laws into
political, civil and criminal categories, but the main thing is to
remember that all laws, whatever their precise form, are rooted
in man's being. 'All the rules of natural right are engraved
more firmly in the hearts of men than in all Justinian's rubbish.
Make men honest and virtuous and I guarantee that they will
know enough law' (III, 1001). This does not eliminate the need
for citizens to be familiar with the laws of their country and the
rules by which they are governed. It is also a particularly bad
habit to allow laws to fall into disuse; any law which is no
longer observed should be abrogated. 'Few laws, but well
digested and especially well observed.' 'Anyone who mentions
a law in a free State mentions a matter which makes the citizen
tremble, and the king first of all.' This is yet another reason for
keeping the laws alive in the citizens' hearts, for as soon as the
laws are deprived of their power, the State is 'irremediably
lost'.

The section devoted to economic reforms continues in
several respects the ideas developed in the Corsican plan. More
especially, Rousseau shows the same hostility to money and
finance. The Poles must make a choice: either follow the
example of the corrupt Europeans whose pursuit of wealth and
luxury makes them 'noisy, brilliant and redoubtable' while
enslaving them; or else form 'a free, peaceful and wise nation
which neither fears nor needs anyone because it is self-
sufficient and happy, with simple manners, sound tastes and a
martial spirit without ambition'. In order to achieve this they

must shun finance — 'a word unknown to ancient governments' (a point already made to the Corsicans) — and develop
agriculture. 'Apply your people to agriculture and the arts
necessary to life, make money contemptible and, if possible,
useless, and in order to effect great things, seek and find more
powerful and reliable resources.' Money, as an intermediary, is
an obstacle to the prosperity which comes from the cultivation
of the fields. Agriculture has the great advantage of using the
physical strength of the nation. 'To keep yourselves free and
happy, it is heads, hearts and arms that are necessary; that is
what makes the strength and prosperity of a people. Systems of
finance make venal souls, and as soon as anyone wants merely
to earn money, he gains more by being a scoundrel than an
honest man ... In a word, money is the weakest and the most
futile incentive I know for making the political machine move
to its goal, and the strongest and surest one for diverting it
from it' (III, 1005).

Rousseau again invokes the example of the Swiss and
repeats the suggestion already made to the Corsicans: that
payment in kind is preferable to money. In Switzerland 'all
public service is performed through *corvées*, the State pays for
almost nothing in money'. The lesson is clear: whenever
money is used, there is always the likelihood of degradation
and corruption. 'You will not find one great evil in morality
and in politics in which money is not involved' (III, 1006).
Again, like the Corsicans, the Poles must make themselves as
independent as possible of foreign trade, which serves only to
subject them to all the evil consequences of financial trans-
actions. True independence, on the other hand, can be won
only by those who are self-reliant: men who wish to be free
must not be 'the slaves of their purse'. The Swiss once again
offer the Poles a sound example of this principle by seeking to
perform many different functions themselves instead of paying
other people to perform them on their behalf. 'They are
soldiers, officers, magistrates, workers: they do everything for
the service of the State and, ever ready to pay with their
persons, they do not need to pay again with their purse.'[7]

This advocacy of a strong sense of civic duty is well brought
out in Rousseau's discussion of the 'military system' that
would suit a reformed Poland. He confesses that it is

impossible to ignore the need for adequate military protection, but as in other aspects of its national life, the country must develop its own distinctive characteristics. Just as it differs from the rest of Europe in its character, government, manners and language, so it should have its own 'military constitution, tactics and discipline, so that it is always itself and not another' (III, 1013). In spite of this, a realistic appraisal of its physical situation will reinforce the conviction that 'the most inviolable law of nature is the law of the strongest'. 'There is no legislation, no constitution exempt from this law.' It is therefore impossible to ensure complete protection from foreign invasion, especially when due consideration is given to the large aggressive neighbours who are constantly threatening Poland's borders. On the other hand, it is sheer folly to dream of undertaking foreign conquest. 'Whoever wants to be free must not want to be a conqueror.' The history of the Romans proves this point: they did not become masters of the world by wars of aggression, but by defending themselves against foreign attacks. It follows therefore that the Poles will not have a paid professional army, for regular troops are the 'plague of Europe' and are responsible for its depopulation. On the other hand, they will not lack defenders, for the true defenders of the State are its own members. 'Every citizen must be a soldier by duty, not by trade. Such was the Romans' military system; such is that of the Swiss today; such must that of any free State and especially of Poland' (III, 1014). As the Swiss so clearly prove, a soldier must not be considered 'as a bandit who, in order to live, sells himself for a few pence a day, but a citizen who serves his country and does his duty'.

Rousseau acknowledges that no human art can prevent the strong attacking the weak, and it is probably pointless to try to resist the physical might of ruthless aggressors; but it is still possible and necessary to build up the citizens' inner strength. 'Leave your country wide open like Sparta, but like Sparta build good citadels in the citizens' hearts.' A country which possesses 'a patriotism and a love of freedom inspired by the virtues inseparable from them' will never be subjugated. The love which 'burns in the citizens' heart' may be subjected to a temporary yoke, but it will never be extinguished. Meanwhile, patriotism can be strengthened when the citizens realize (as in so many other activities) that they are carrying out their tasks and duties before the eyes of the public. Nothing can be done without the support of 'public esteem' and this 'patriotic exaltation which lifts men above themselves'.

In a large state like Poland it will not be possible to establish an egalitarian society, even to the extent that it was feasible to do so in Corsica. There will be different orders and class divisions, especially in a society which still contains so many serfs. Yet the essential step is to allow room for movement from one class to another; serfs must be permitted to obtain freedom and burghers to become nobles. Promotion should be based solely on merit and Rousseau envisages the formation of three categories of Poles, who will be distinguished by the wearing of different metal badges bearing appropriate Latin inscriptions! The essential point is for the lowest grades to be inspired by such zeal and enthusiasm that there will be a steady movement upwards. 'Each one sees before him the road free for him to attain every goal, and everybody, while serving the fatherland, gradually moves towards the most honourable ranks and virtue opens the doors which fortune likes to close' (III, 1029).

In these last pages Rousseau offers the Poles the vision of a reformed fatherland sustained by ardent patriotism. As elsewhere in his political writings, he puts his final emphasis on inner strength rather than on complicated laws. As for their future, the Poles must realise the futility of trying to protect themselves by elaborate treaties. European governments concerned with nothing but their selfish interests will never understand 'what incentives the love of the fatherland and the impulse of virtue gives to free souls' (III, 1038). Even so, Rousseau thinks that the Poles can confidently accept his proposals, for these are suitable not only to the particular needs of their nation but are, in a much wider sense, 'adapted to the human heart'.

7. Philosophy and the Individual

Rousseau intended *Emile* and the *Social Contract* to complete his authorship and, in fact, the few formal works produced after 1762 were the result of special circumstances: the constitutions for Corsica and Poland were specifically requested by representatives of those nations; the *Letter to M. de Beaumont* was a reply to the Archbishop of Paris's condemnation of the *Profession of Faith of the Savoyard Priest*; and the polemical *Letters Written from the Mountain* were prompted by the Genevan authorities' attack upon the *Social Contract*. Useful though they are for the clarification of particular aspects of Rousseau's philosophy, these works do not add substantially to its essential principles. The main emphasis of his later literary activities falls elsewhere: on the personal writings which spanned the last fourteen years of his life. Their origin was quite different from that of the earlier didactic works, for they were concerned almost exclusively with an analysis of his own life and character. As such they constitute a new confessional genre which was to have far-reaching effects upon later literary generations. At the same time it has to be recognized that, although they do not fit easily into the formal pattern of Rousseau's philosophy, these personal writings are very relevant to an account of his work as a whole; as well as dealing with a new personal theme, they contain a number of echoes of the principles elaborated in the didactic works.

The genesis of the first of the personal writings — the four letters written to M. de Malesherbes in January 1762 — is very clearly related to the tensions of Rousseau's inner life. His publisher Rey had already wanted to use the story of his life as an introduction to a general edition of his works (*CC*, IX, 149, 359), while a clergyman friend called Moultou made the same suggestion in 1761. When in September 1762 Rey repeated his request, Rousseau complained that he did not have the leisure or peace of mind necessary for the completion of such a task.

141

'For six months my life has unfortunately been a work of importance requiring time and reflection' (*CC*, XIII, 136; XIV, 55). Meanwhile, the first piece of personal writing had been brought into being by the distress and anxiety associated with the publication of *Emile*. Rousseau's decision to make this his last work was accompanied by the firm determination that it should be his finest. Although he had frequently quarrelled with his publisher Marc-Michel Rey, he had become attached to him and, whatever their differences, had not doubted his essential honesty. However, Rousseau's protectress, Mme de Luxembourg, convinced that he could obtain a better financial reward from his work, undertook to arrange for the publication of *Emile* in Paris. Unfortunately, when Rousseau heard nothing from the publishers, he became convinced that a sinister plot was afoot to produce his book in a mutilated form. His anxieties were undoubtedly increased by a distressing accident: a catheter broke off in his urethra and caused him considerable pain and discomfort. His growing consciousness of being at odds with his age made him identify himself all the more readily with *Emile*, which became for him a kind of objective embodiment of his own better self: into it he had put all his idealism and his noblest thoughts about the nature of man, so that the destruction or mutilation of the book would be the same as an attack upon his own inner being. All his life he had been preoccupied with the problem of arbitrary power and in existing society he saw the weak and poor being put at the mercy of the powerful and rich. He was now convinced that one of the most sinister and powerful bodies of contemporary religious life, the Jesuits, were in the plot to publish a false version of his book which, instead of bringing him respect and glory, would lead to nothing but ignominy and shame. Since he had decided to incorporate into *Emile* a statement of his beliefs — the *Profession of Faith of the Savoyard Priest* — it was perhaps natural that he should attach particular importance to this part of the work and let his imagination become obsessed with the very organisation which was for him the symbol of ruthless ecclesiastical power. Thanks largely to the intervention of the sensible and kindly Lamoignon de Malesherbes, the minister responsible for book publication and sympathetic to the new 'philosophical' movement, Rousseau's fears were

142

finally allayed, but he was left with a deep regret at having unjustly vilified his publishers' reputation; he attributed his actions to his 'frightened imagination' which, he asserted, had been stimulated by his loneliness, his friends' silence and the publishers' carelessness. It was perhaps this episode which impelled him to write to Malesherbes — 'a man for whom I had much esteem' — in order to efface the unfavourable impression left by his earlier conduct; he wanted, as he says in the *Confessions*, to explain the true motives of his conduct as well as 'his tastes, inclinations and character and all that took place in his heart'.

His four letters to Malesherbes form an indispensable introduction to the later personal writings, for they clearly reveal one of Rousseau's main reasons for composing them: the need to destroy the false image of himself which he believes to exist in the minds of other people.[1] His withdrawal from society, he avers, is not due to vanity or misanthropy; in spite of his genuine hatred of injustice and wickedness, he has abandoned society because of a 'natural love of solitude' which 'has only increased as he came to know men better' and has made him prefer the 'chimerical beings' created by his imagination to the company of real people. His recent aberrations have not sprung from discontent with his present situation, but from 'a disordered imagination ready to take fright at everything and to carry everything to extremes'. His aversion to Parisian life is due to his 'love of freedom' — but he admits that this freedom owes more to laziness than to pride, since he has always been irked by the petty habits and duties of society. His constant desire is for a spontaneous uninhibited friendship involving neither obligation nor gratitude; 'You follow your heart and all is done.' True happiness consists of 'not doing what you do not want to do' rather than of 'doing what you want to'. His seclusion, therefore, is based solely on his need to enjoy his immediate existence.

In these letters to Malesherbes he has one main purpose: 'I shall describe myself to you as I am'. He does not fear to do this since he believes that 'of all the men he has known in his life, none was better than he'. By goodness, however, Rousseau does not mean virtue: a good man follows his natural innate impulses while the virtuous man relies on the strength of his will. If Rousseau is good, he is not necessarily virtuous, for his 'lazy soul' is not capable of sustained effort. In everything he obeys the inclination of his sensitivity which makes him oscillate between lethargy and ardent feeling. He goes on to explain this contradiction by referring to the unconventional upbringing which subjected him to the influence of 'a heroic and romantic taste', for from an early age, as we have seen,[2] his reading of Plutarch and of sentimental novels made it difficult for him to accept the real world.

All this has had a decisive effect upon his attitude towards his literary work. After describing the inspiration which led to the composition of his first *Discourse*, he points out that he could never write for mercenary motives but only in order to express deeply felt convictions. In no sense a professional writer, he did not pay heed to public opinion or let himself be dominated by contemporary tastes; his personal reform was due to his need to free himself from a corrupting environment, so that any work subsequently produced would contain the sincere and uninhibited formulation of ideas intended for the betterment of his fellow-men.

He insists that his desire to escape from the presence of tyrannical friends who want to make him happy, as he puts it, in their fashion and not in his, makes him realise that, in spite of his 'loving heart', he can be 'self-sufficient'. This would seem to be the cause of his inner conflict, for his 'natural love of solitude' was not strong enough to overcome his need for the affection of others. As he was wont to say, his heart was 'devoured by the need to love and be loved' and he even admitted later that 'I should love society as much as others do if I were not sure of showing myself not only to my disadvantage but quite different from what I am' (I, 116). To Malesherbes he is content to say that his love of men is too great for him to need to choose among them: 'I love them all'. Yet it is clear that his rejection of particular men or groups is prompted by a fear of being dominated by them. 'I cannot conceal from you that I have a violent aversion for conditions which dominate others... I hate the great, I hate their condition, hardness, prejudices, pettiness and all their vices: I should hate them much more if I despised them less.' Nevertheless, he admits to having been won over by the Maréchal and

Maréchale de Luxembourg, to whom he is now completely devoted, his only regret being that their social status and his own particular position make it impossible for them to achieve complete personal equality. How pleasant it would have been if the Maréchal had been a simple country gentleman and Jean-Jacques an ordinary man without literary talent!

The third — and most lyrical — letter shows how the difficulty of establishing firm relations with other people made him turn more and more to the resources of his inner life and a new awareness of the physical world. He describes his habit of taking lonely walks in the midst of nature, where he would 'enjoy himself, the whole universe, all that is, all that can be and all the beauty of the world of sense, imagination and intellect. I would gather around me all that flattered my heart; my desire would be the measure of my pleasures. No, never have voluptuaries known such delights. I have enjoyed my day-dreams a hundred times more than they have enjoyed reality.' Particularly satisfying were the occasions when he would get up at dawn to contemplate 'the whole of nature and its inconceivable author'. When he had completed his obligations for the day, he would seek some corner of the forest which bore no trace of human enslavement or domination, 'some refuge which I believed I was the first to enter and where no importunate third party would intervene between nature and me'. There he would experience a renewal of his being and let himself be so completely carried away by the colourful profusion and variety of trees, plants and flowers that he could not help recalling Jesus's saying that 'Solomon in all his glory was not arrayed like one of these'.

Soon his imagination would add to his pleasure by populating this beautiful scene with beings worthy of living in it; he would 'create a golden age after his liking'. Suddenly, however, he would be saddened by 'the nothingness of his day-dreams'. 'Even if all my dreams had turned into realities, I should have imagined, dreamed, desired yet more. I found within myself an inexplicable void which nothing could have filled; a certain heart-felt longing for another kind of enjoyment, of which I had no idea, but of which I felt the need. Well! that too was enjoyment, since I was pervaded by a very active feeling and by an alluring sadness of which I should not have liked to be deprived' (I, 1140). This remarkable expression of the gap between possibility and reality, between the infinite longing of his soul and the physical limitations of the finite natural world recalls in certain respects the mood of Julie, who had not been able to find satisfaction in earthly happiness. In her case, however, the situation had been complicated by the pressure of an unfulfilled love, so that she did not turn to the physical world but to the thought of the next life. Jean-Jacques, on the other hand, is not willing to remain absorbed in a mere sense of absence and nothingness but seeks out the infinite spiritual dimension of the universe itself. The final mood is one of pleasure and not of anguish, for his complete absorption in the experience does not make him lose the capacity for enjoying the infinite resources of his own consciousness, in spite of his reference to the 'inexplicable void' and the 'nothingness' of his dreams, Rousseau is convinced that he has at last found 'his life's true happiness, a happiness without bitterness, vexations and regrets, and to which he would willingly have limited his existence'. Indeed he believes that eternity itself cannot offer anything better than these 'ravishing contemplations'.

The letters to Malesherbes were followed by a much more extensive and elaborate attempt to describe and analyse Rousseau's true character as he himself saw it — the *Confessions*, which were begun in 1766 and completed about 1770. The later parts of this work were written at a time when Rousseau was suffering from intense emotional stress and many a page is darkened by the shadows of the persistent and deep-rooted conviction that he was the victim of a universal plot aimed at vilifying and humiliating him. The complex psychological aspects of his obsession with persecution having been examined elsewhere,[3] it will be sufficient to stress here the main features of the *Confessions* themselves rather than their genesis and background. The mere length of the work already shows that Rousseau is still aware of his need to destroy the false image of himself which he believes to exist in other people's minds. Now, however, he is not content to follow the fairly summary mode of presentation characteristic of the letters to Malesherbes; he proposes to let the portrait emerge from a detailed account of his life from which no significant feature will be excluded.

Some very valuable indications of the ultimate purpose of the *Confessions* are to be found in the first introduction, which was subsequently suppressed in favour of the short preamble added to the final version. From the very outset he makes it clear that the good and innocent Jean-Jacques cannot emerge until the false image existing in other people's minds has been completely destroyed. This preoccupation, already apparent in the earlier letters to Malesherbes, plays a vital part in the inspiration of the *Confessions*. 'People have made of me', he writes in the first introduction, 'only an imaginary and fantastic being' (I, 1152). 'Everyone has fashioned me according to his own fancy.' More particularly, people have judged him to be a harsh, misanthropic man insensitive to the needs and feelings of others. The only effective way to dispel this error is to produce a portrait unmatched for its frankness and sincerity. This is a point very forcibly made in the final preamble. 'I am carrying out an enterprise which has no precedent and the execution of which will have no imitator'. 'This is the only human portrait, painted exactly according to nature and in all its truth, which exists and probably will ever exist' (I, 2).

The uniqueness of this self-portrait is not due solely to its creator's exceptional honesty, but also to his exceptional character. 'I feel my heart and I know men. I am made like none of those whom I have seen; I dare to believe that I am made like none of those who exist. If I am not better, I am at least different' (I, 5). In spite of this claim to uniqueness, Rousseau is careful to indicate that this is not merely an eccentric and idiosyncratic portrait, but one that has been made according to *nature*. He also speaks of 'truth' as a criterion that goes beyond mere individual whims. As the subsequent account makes clear, the claim to be unique is connected with his belief that other men have been corrupted by their artificial environment. Jean-Jacques alone has been able to preserve the truth of nature, largely because of his unusual temperament: being a man of sensitivity rather than of reason, he insists that he has never lost his essentially child-like nature. This 'primitive' view of himself is one to which he frequently returns. 'I was born a child and still remain one in many respects'. His simple, almost naïve character is something which his contemporaries — the victims of subtle and devious influences imposed on them by their corrupt environment — will never understand. Even so, the *Confessions*, by the very fact of showing a man in 'all the truth of nature', are intended as a challenge to all other men to examine their own characters in the light of what they now read; the work is meant to be a standard or criterion — *une pièce de comparaison* — by which other men can be led to examine their own real being; this 'unique and useful work' will be henceforth indispensable to the serious 'study of man'.

The curious amalgamation of personal preoccupation and didactic intent is well brought out by the apocalyptic tone of the third paragraph of the text. All readers, he avers, will be finally called upon to pronounce judgement on Jean-Jacques and by that very act they will also be impelled to judge themselves. 'Let the trump of the last judgement sound whenever it will, I shall come with this book in my hand, and present myself to the sovereign judge.' Since Jean-Jacques has 'unveiled his inner being as God himself has seen it', he asks Him to summon 'the countless multitude of his fellow-men', so that they too can make an important decision. 'Let each one of them, in his turn, unveil his heart at the feet of thy throne with the same sincerity and then let a single one of them say to thee, if he dares: "I was better than that man"' (I, 5).

In spite of this broad human intention, the emphasis of the *Confessions* is clearly upon the individual rather than upon the universal aspect of Rousseau's character. This is made very apparent in his discussion of the problem of writing an autobiography and his own method of resolving it. Rousseau is not of course unaware of predecessors in this 'confessional' field, even though he believes that they have all fallen short of his own uncompromising earnestness and frankness. Apart from St Augustine, whose personal confessions were subordinated to a theological purpose, Rousseau mentions the Italian writer Jerome Cardan (Cardano) who was 'so mad that no benefit can be derived from his reveries'. Montaigne is considered to be a worthier example, but Rousseau charges him with partiality. 'Montaigne depicts himself in a good likeness, but in profile. Who knows whether some scar on his cheek or a blinded eye on the side he is hiding from us, would not have completely changed his features?' (I, 1150). In other words,

Montaigne was eager to present only a favourable self-portrait, whereas Jean-Jacques has 'shown himself as he is: contemptible and base when I have been so; good, generous and sublime also ... I shall loudly say: that is what I have done, thought and been. I have uttered the good and the bad with the same frankness, I have not kept silent about the bad or added anything good' (I, 5).

Rousseau considers that the chronological method of character portrayal has the great advantage of offering his readers the material from which they can form their own authentic portrait of him. It is not easy to present a static, full-length portrait because 'the succession of affections and ideas' is constantly modifying those which follow, so that the 'chain of effects' has to be traced back to the 'first causes'. 'I should like in some way', explains Rousseau at the end of his fourth book, 'to make my soul transparent to the reader's eyes and, to do that, I seek to show it to him from every point of view, to reveal it in every light and to act in such a way that there is not a movement which he cannot perceive, so that he can judge by himself the principle which produces it' (I, 175). In this way it is the reader who will have the ultimate responsibility of deciding the main features of Jean-Jacques's character. 'It is up to him to assemble these elements and to determine the being which is constituted by them.'

Another factor impelling Rousseau towards critical self-examination was the knowledge that he had often behaved in a strangely unpredictable manner; whilst decisively rejecting others' false interpretation of his behaviour, he admits that his character contains some disconcertingly unusual features and that he himself has not always been able to understand the true reasons for his behaviour. On several occasions he has acted so irrationally that he has seemed 'another man' and 'unlike himself'. It is therefore not surprising if other people, who see only the outward appearance, have failed to understand his real being, for his actions have often been at variance with his inner feelings and contrary to his real nature. This unusual conduct may have occasionally raised him to 'sublime' heights —for example, the inspiration of the first *Discourse* allowed him 'to see another universe and to become another man' — but at other times 'these inconceivable moments of delirium when he was no longer himself' have plunged him into depths of unprecedented baseness. He always retained, for example, a vividly painful memory of the occasion when he accused the servant-girl Marion of a theft which he himself had committed. He recalls yet another shameful episode when he abandoned his old music-master, Lemaître, who had been struck down by a fit in the streets of Lyon. Still more serious and persistent was the thought that he had abandoned his own illegitimate children to a Foundlings' Home. As he admits in the course of his narrative, memories such as these formed one of the main reasons for the composition of the *Confessions*; he had an overwhelming need to alleviate an intolerable burden of guilt by revealing to others the details of his past misdeeds.

In order to explain such uncharacteristic behaviour, Rousseau believed that it was necessary to go beyond the actual circumstances of these incidents and to examine their hidden motives. This means that, although the *Confessions* assume an autobiographical form, they are not meant to be the mere story of his life. 'I am not writing the history of the events in themselves as much as that of the state of my soul when they occurred.' Facts are only 'occasional causes' intended to reveal the 'chain of secret affections'; he is seeking to retrace the 'thread of his secret dispositions' and 'the secret history of his soul' (I, 1155); he is proposing to study 'the apparent effect of which the inner cause is hidden and often very complicated'. Many important moments of his life are thus described from a double point of view; the external circumstances and outward behaviour on the one side and, on the other, the inner feelings and motives ultimately determining them.

The episode concerning the servant-girl Marion is a good example. First of all Rousseau narrates the incident itself and he then adds the 'true' explanation. After his abjuration of Protestantism at the Hospice for Catechumens at Turin in 1728, he worked for a time as a lackey in the service of a wealthy widow, Mme de Vercellis, who was dying of cancer. Her death soon led to the break-up of the household and this involved Rousseau in a crime which left him with 'an unbearable weight of remorse' for the rest of his life. One day it was found that a small ribbon mentioned in the household inventory was missing. Jean-Jacques had taken it, but as he had not made any serious effort to hide it, it was soon discovered and he was accused of the theft. He, in turn, immediately accused a pretty, fresh-looking young servant-girl called Marion of having stolen the ribbon. When Mme de Vercellis's nephew the Comte de la Roque investigated the matter, Rousseau persisted in his accusation. Marion quietly but firmly protested her innocence, urging Jean-Jacques to 'withdraw into himself and not dishonour an innocent girl who had never done him any harm'. With an 'infernal impudence' and 'diabolical audacity', Rousseau persisted in his lie in spite of a 'look which would have disarmed the demons'. Unable to solve the problem, the count dismissed both servants with the remark that 'the conscience of the guilty one would sufficiently avenge the innocent' (I, 85). Tormented ever afterwards by the wrong he had done and especially by the terrible fate that might have subsequently befallen the innocent Marion, Rousseau confessed that 'this cruel memory sometimes disturbs and upsets me to the point of seeing in my insomnias this poor girl coming to reproach me for my crime as though it were only yesterday' (I, 85-6). In spite of the severe condemnation to which most people who knew only the material facts would subject him, Rousseau insists that his action was not due to wickedness but rather to his liking for the girl. 'I accused her of having done what I wanted to do and of having given me the ribbon because my intention was to give it to her.' The presence of other people with their accusing looks filled him with 'a shame which he feared more than any punishment — more than death, more than crime, more than anything in the world'. He could not bear the thought of being 'publicly declared, in my presence, a thief, liar and slanderer'. If the count had taken him aside privately and urged him to tell the truth, Rousseau insists that he would have done so. His only hope was that 'forty years of uprightness and honour' had been a partial atonement for this youthful crime.

In spite of the limited validity of such an 'explanation' of aberrant behaviour, Rousseau was certainly ahead of his time in his earnest effort to uncover deeper and only partially conscious motives. While he was not a direct precursor of Freud, he anticipated some of the findings of modern psychology. Apart from his analysis of guilty episodes such as those just mentioned, Rousseau did not hesitate to speak frankly about his sexual deviations. He believed that his submissive attitude towards women and his inability to make any positive advances to them were due largely to the precocious stimulation of his sexual feelings by the chastisement administered to him by Mlle Lambercier, the sister of the clergyman to whose care he was entrusted in his early years; he describes the masochistic pleasure he derived from being spanked by her: 'I had found in the pain and even in the shame an element of sexuality which left me with more desire than fear to experience it again by the same hand' (I, 15). He was so deeply stirred by his experience that 'it was thereafter impossible for me to be sexually aggressive with women'. 'To be at the knees of an imperious mistress, to obey her orders and to have to ask forgiveness of her was for me very sweet enjoyment and the more my lively imagination inflamed my blood, the more did I assume the appearance of a bashful lover' (I, 17). Subsequently, he 'possessed few women but he none the less enjoyed many in his own way; that is, through his imagination'. In spite of a 'blood burning with sensuality' and a 'combustible temperament', he could not act aggressively towards women and was content to transform them into 'so many Mlle Lamberciers'.

Rousseau's account also makes it clear that this incipient masochism had been prepared by the psychological development of his early childhood. As a young child he had a desperate need to be the object of other people's affection. 'To be loved by all that surrounded me was the keenest of my desires' (I, 14), and for a short time he felt that his life was based on the security of 'tender, affectionate and peaceful feelings'. The growing complexity of his sexual reactions is also shown by his contradictory reactions to two girls mentioned in the *Confessions* — Mlle de Vulson and Mlle Goton. While he wanted to keep such a tyrannical hold upon the former that he could not bear any other male to approach her, he had intimate little meetings with the latter, who spoke to him 'like a schoolmistress' and subdued him with her 'imposing proud look'; she took 'great privaties with him while allowing him to take none with her, treating him exactly like a child.' He felt that Mlle de Vulson's endearments, on the other hand, appealed more to his heart than to his senses. Even so, he was completely devoted to both of them and could not think of one without the other. Enjoying an untroubled emotion and a 'calm joy' in Mlle de Vulson's presence, he was completely overwhelmed by his feelings for Mlle Goton, for whom 'he would have thrown himself into the flames, had she so ordered' (I, 29). These contradictory attitudes did not exclude an early aversion to the physical reality of sex of which, in his earliest years, he had 'an odious and disgusting image' associated with the coupling of dogs. Since, however, his sexual desire was too strong to be ignored, he was impelled later on to separate sex from any truly amorous feeling towards real women. His only permanent sexual relationship, which he himself terminated in early middle-age, was with an ignorant servant-girl. At other times he would relieve his 'erotic furies' by masturbation — a lifelong habit which he was never able to overcome, for, as he acknowledged, it allowed him to satisfy all his sexual and emotional craving without involving him in the emotional complications of a relationship with a real woman.

The direct expression of sexual need was impeded by his great shyness, to which he often refers. He speaks, for example, of his 'unconquerably foolish, sullen shyness, which was rooted in his fear of falling short of good manners'. He often mentions his 'accursed' shyness which made him appear to be a 'rather foolish character', even in the presence of 'people who were as stupid as himself'. This diffidence obviously affected his attitude towards women. Unable to confront them directly, he would seek to engage their attention by devious means. As an adolescent he indulged for a time in exhibitionism, exposing his naked posterior to young women, probably in the hope that they would be sexually aroused by such a sight or at least make some move towards him!

While giving a detailed description of such abnormal behaviour, Rousseau explains that his intense need to transform himself into the object of another's affectionate regard did not exclude a more assertive, even aggressive role: emotional dependence could alternate with powerful self-affirmation. Already at an early age he seems to have considered himself as a 'redresser of wrongs'. When he saw someone being made the victim of injustice, he would be fired with violent, almost sadistic hostility towards the wrong-doer. On one occasion he threw himself between his father and brother when the latter was being severely chastised (I, 9-10). Likewise, he rushed to the defence of his cousin Abraham when he became the butt of other children's mockery. Throughout his life Rousseau describes incidents in which extreme anger and indignation were aroused by some act of apparent injustice, especially when the weak were being oppressed by the strong. Very revealing is his observation that he could sometimes feel the same passionate concern for people, long since dead, about whom he was merely reading. Whenever 'he read of the cruelties of a fierce tyrant, or the subtle atrocities of a rascally priest, he would willingly go and stab these wretches even though he were to perish a hundred times in the act' (I, 20). In adult life his aggression was often given a purely emotional or imaginative expression and did not lead to any direct physical action, although it made him see himself more and more as the innocent and unhappy victim of another's wrong-doing. At the same time this resentment against the powerful and strong did not exclude an almost resigned acceptance that such oppression was an inevitable aspect of social and political life.

The way in which a psychological shock can influence a man's subsequent moral outlook is very well brought out in the shattering experience of injustice that occurred during Rousseau's stay with the Lamberciers. Mlle Lambercier — 'a person whom I loved like a mother and perhaps more' — one day accused him of having broken one of her combs. His persistent protestations of innocence did not prevent him from being adjudged guilty and forced to endure 'the rigour of a frightful punishment for a crime I had not committed'. More anguishing than the physical pain were the 'indignation, fury, and despair' provoked by the unfounded accusation. It was a decisive moment in his life and yet an injustice for which even the instigator was not responsible. 'Appearances', he admits, 'condemned me', for Mlle Lambercier was no doubt genuinely convinced of his guilt. Nevertheless, he felt that his soul had been scarred for ever. 'This feeling of violence and injustice has remained so deeply engraved in my soul that all the ideas connected with it revive my first emotion; and this feeling, relating to me in its origin, has assumed such firmness in itself and has become so detached from any personal interest, that my heart flares up at the sight or sound of any unjust act, whatever may be its object and in whatever place, as if the effect devolved on me' (I, 20).

The originality of the *Confessions* is not restricted to Rousseau's psychological insights, for the work was not due to a single motive. As well as being a search for self-knowledge and self-justification, it was also a sustained attempt to recapture the happiness of the past. The very fact that, in his later years, Rousseau became increasingly obsessed by the thought that he was the object of universal hostility thrust him back into himself and made him find there resources which he believed were not available to him in the outside world. He constantly laments the brevity of past happiness, but he also stresses its ecstatic quality. As he feels the darkness closing in, he dwells with increasing pleasure upon the happy moments of the past. In particular, he likes to savour once again the memories of his childhood, and all the more readily as he retains a profound belief in the persistence of his child-like character. The sombre moments of his sojourn with the Lamberciers did not prevent him from seeing this period of his life as an 'earthly paradise'. With them he lived at Bossey a few miles from Geneva and he had as his companion his cousin Abraham, to whom he became closely attached. 'The simplicity of this rural life' was very appealing, not only because it opened his eyes to the beauties of nature and so left an indelible impression on his mind, but also because it gave him his first experience of friendship: Abraham was a very congenial companion who shared his happiness. 'Always inseparable, we were self-sufficient' (I, 25). 'Friendship filled our hearts so completely that it was sufficient for us to be together for the simplest tastes to be our delight' (I, 26). They seemed to be living in an 'earthly paradise' beneath the gaze of 'gods who read into their hearts'. This idea of a self-sufficient intimacy in the presence of superior but benevolent beings was to represent one of Rousseau's most persistent longings.

A particular strong lyrical tone pervades the account of his life with Mme de Warens. With her he found an emotional security he had never previously known: he enjoyed 'the charm of a happy life' and spent 'happy, quiet' days marked by a deep feeling of 'innocence'. The experience had a quasi-religious quality as his language reveals. 'My heart which was still new abandoned itself to everything with a child-like pleasure or rather, I dare to say, with an angelic delight; for in truth these quiet enjoyments have the serenity of those of paradise' (I, 244). He does not hesitate to say that in the presence of Mme de Warens he felt as though his heart was 'open to God'. 'I had neither transport nor desire with her; I was in a ravishing calm, enjoying without knowing what. I should have passed my life in this way and even eternity itself without being bored for a single moment' (I, 107).

His affection for Mme de Warens was enhanced by the rural setting in which they lived. 'The song of the birds, the beauty of the day, the gentleness of the landscape, the scattered rural houses in which I imagined our common dwelling-place, all that struck me with such a lively, tender, sad and touching expression that I saw myself as it were ecstatically transported to that happy time and to that happy abode where my heart, possessing all the bliss that it could want, savoured it in inexpressible raptures, without even thinking of the pleasure of the senses' (I, 108). It was sometimes difficult for him to separate his feelings for Mme de Warens from his enjoyment of nature. 'I saw her everywhere among the flowers and the verdure: her charms and those of spring were mingled in my eyes. My heart, hitherto restricted, found more room in this space and my sighs were breathed more freely among these orchards' (I, 105). They found a particular pleasure in walking together in the countryside where they could indulge in their expansive feelings. He recalled one specific occasion, when 'a fresh breeze moved the leaves, the air was pure, the horizon cloudless; serenity reigned in heaven as it did in our hearts' (I, 244), as though it were a 'waking dream'.

The feeling for nature is present in many parts of the *Confessions*, especially in Rousseau's description of his youthful years. Apart from his life with Mme de Warens, he also likes to recall moments when he was alone in the midst of nature. He describes a particularly delightful night he spent near the river at Lyon. 'I was walking in a kind of ecstasy giving my senses and heart to all that, and only sighing a little at the regret of

enjoying it alone' (I, 169). He also delighted in wilder landscapes enlivened by torrents, waterfalls, tall fir-trees and
precipitous cliffs, while he obtained great emotional satisfaction from being close to stretches of clear water; he always
retained a particularly strong liking for the lake of Geneva. As
he walked along amid so much beauty, he 'disposed like a
master of the whole of nature; my heart wandering from one
object to another, unites and identifies with those which flatter
it, surrounds itself with charming images, is intoxicated with
delightful feelings' (I, 162).

Sometimes these descriptions of nature serve as a background for some particularly appealing incident, as on the
occasion when he met the two charming girls with whom he
spent an unforgettable day — the so-called idyll of the cherries.
'How I love to dwell from time to time on the pleasant
moments of my youth!' (I, 134). He recalls one fine summer
day when he had got up early to see the beauty of the sunrise
and the countryside. By chance he met two girls, Mlle de
Graffenried and Mlle Galley, who were trying to cross a stream
with their horses. After accepting his help, they laughingly
made him their 'prisoner' and took him with them to Mlle
Galley's *château* at Toune, where they spent a delightful day
dining and disporting themselves; Jean-Jacques found particular pleasure in climbing a cherry-tree in the orchard and
throwing down the fruit to the girls below. He vividly evokes
the joyful innocence of an occasion that 'moved and charmed'
him more than any other pleasure he ever experienced. If he
had any amorous feeling for the two girls, he knew that he need
not fear to give way to it. 'The sweet memory of this day cost
the girls nothing; the tender union which prevailed among the
three of us was equal to much livelier pleasures and could not
have subsisted with them; we loved one another without
mystery and shame, and we wanted to love one another for
ever thus' (I, 138).

Although Rousseau often complained of his lack of memory
for the ordinary things of life, he had a remarkable gift for
recalling details of the experiences and emotions appertaining
to his happy past. He himself insists that he had a vivid
recollection of 'all the circumstances, places, people and times'
of his life at Bossey. Similarly, when describing his years with

Mme de Warens, he says: 'Not only do I recall the times, places and people, but all the surrounding objects, the temperature of the air, its smell and colour, a certain local impression which was felt only there and the vividness of which again carries me away' (I, 122). Moreover, even in this psychological area, Rousseau is again ahead of his time, for he was aware of the power of involuntary and 'affective' memory, as is clear from his association of the memory of Mme de Warens with the sight of a periwinkle seen many years later (I, 226) — a detail which some critics have seen as anticipating the famous involuntary memory discussed by Proust.

In many parts of the *Confessions* Rousseau shows himself to have been a prose-poet in an age which was singularly lacking in lyrical inspiration. He himself was aware of the linguistic and stylistic problem of recording impressions and feelings which often escape direct analysis and description. 'For what I have to say,' he writes in his first introduction, 'it would be necessary to invent a language as new as my project: for what tone, what style must be used in order to sort out this huge chaos of such diverse and contradictory, often such base and sometimes such sublime feelings as those with which I was constantly stirred? How many trifles, how many mere no-things must I not set forth, into what revolting, indecent and often ridiculous details must I not enter, in order to follow the thread of my secret dispositions, to show how each impression which has left its mark on my soul came into it for the first time?... I shall not try to make my style uniform; I shall always have the style which comes to me, I shall unhesitatingly change it according to my mood, I shall tell each thing as I feel and see it, without affectation or constraint, without worrying about the medley. By giving myself at the same time to the memory of the impression received and to the present feeling, I shall doubly depict the state of my soul, namely, at the moment when the event happened to me and at the moment when I described it: my uneven and natural style, now rapid and now diffuse, now wise and now mad, now serious and now gay, will itself form part of my story' (I, 1153-4).

Since Rousseau intended the *Confessions* to challenge his readers to deliver their verdict upon him, it seemed that in 1770 his wish would be granted, for he was invited to read the work in a number of aristocratic houses. Friends and writers were also present at other readings and have left their reminiscences of them. Rousseau, however, was upset by their reactions: some were disconcerted, others shocked or deeply moved, nobody was prepared to give his opinion. 'Everybody was silent' (I, 656). This reticence was perhaps not unexpected in a society still dominated by aristocratic traditions of decorum and good manners. The gradual increase of *sensibilité* in the eighteenth century still remained a predominantly middle-class phenomenon and, in any case, was more literary than social in its expression. Society was as unprepared to receive an intimately personal work like the *Confessions* as it was incapable of understanding the strangely tormented character of the man who had written it. On his side, Jean-Jacques tended to treat his audience as an element in a complex relationship he was trying to establish within himself: he wanted those present to confirm him in his claim that he was indeed the good and innocent Jean-Jacques he professed to be.

Any hope that these readings would effectively destroy the false Jean-Jacques existing in other people's minds was thwarted by the action of the Parisian police-chief Sartine to whom Rousseau's erstwhile friends, apprehensive about what he might have said about them in the *Confessions*, made strong protests. When Sartine placed a ban on further readings, Rousseau was thrust back into himself, his doubts and fears being exacerbated by yet another seemingly incontrovertible proof of his enemies' relentless malevolence. This crisis prompted him to search desperately for a more effective and direct means of self-portrayal. Although he was still faced with the problem of circumventing his enemies' devious tactics, he was determined to find a method of presentation that left no room for uncertainty.

It was probably these considerations which finally induced him to begin another major piece of personal writing — the *Dialogues: Rousseau Judge of Jean-Jacques* — on which he worked for four years, completing it in 1776. The two interlocutors are 'Rousseau', an apparently detached but critical observer who is anxious to discover the truth about the Jean-Jacques case, and the 'Frenchman', an honest but gullible member of the public who has taken at its face-value the monstrous image of Jean-Jacques disseminated by his enemies. The real issue, however, is between characters who, though not appearing directly, are the main subject of discussion: Jean-Jacques and the 'gentlemen' responsible for the plot against him. The inordinately long and repetitive conversation, which extends through three dialogues, returns with obsessive persistence to the notion of the universal plot against Jean-Jacques. Although the work for the most part reads like a paranoid nightmare, it is occasionally illuminated by remarkable flashes of insight as Rousseau reveals new facets of his character or discusses significant aspects of his work.

It soon becomes clear that the medium of the dialogue, though purporting to provide the reader with an impartial account of the case, is merely a device for presenting a verdict that has been decided from the very outset. The false image of the wicked, scheming Rousseau who is constantly trying to hide his true character finally gives way to that of the 'man of nature' who has not changed much in the course of his life and whose mode of existence is in complete conformity with his character. 'Of all the men I have known', says Rousseau, 'the one whose character derives most fully from his temperament alone is Jean-Jacques. He is what nature made him; education has modified him only very little' (I, 799-800). Far from being a subtle adult, he is merely 'an old child' — a simple, impulsive being whose unaffected goodness has made him the object of his enemies' 'anxious, vigilant eyes' (I, 951). Alive or dead, he is — and always will be — a disturbing figure for evil-doers.

As soon as the *Dialogues* were finished, Rousseau was faced with the problem of deciding what to do with the manuscript, for he did not believe that it could be published in his lifetime. He was also convinced that a man who, like himself, was the object of a universal conspiracy would have difficulty in finding a reliable friend to whom his precious *dépôt* could be entrusted. After approaching the philosopher Condillac, who, to Rousseau's dismay, discussed the work in purely literary terms, and another confidant, a young Englishman called Brooke Boothby, who promised to take care of the manuscript, Rousseau was seized with doubts. He finally decided to trust only in Providence. Reflection upon divine power led him to consider the supreme instrument of earthly power, the king.

Since, in his political works, Rousseau had reluctantly conceded that a monarchy might be the only feasible form of government for large states, it was not unreasonable for him to assume that the king was the most influential figure in French society. Rousseau fervently hoped that, if the *Dialogues* could eventually reach the monarch, the latter would ensure the safety of the manuscript and see that justice was done. In Rousseau's mind the association of the divine father and the royal father did not exclude the idea of a mother-figure. It will be recalled that Rousseau's religious outlook, when imaginatively expressed, included a feminine principle and that Julie, the heroine of *La Nouvelle Héloïse*, appears at times to embody the characteristics of a female Christ. The feminine principle, the divine mother, Mother Church, these were effectively to be found in Paris itself — in the great cathedral of Notre Dame. It was on the high altar of this church that Jean-Jacques decided to place his manuscript. Unfortunately he soon discovered that Providence was not looking kindly upon him, for when he entered the cathedral on Christmas Eve 1776, he found that the iron grill protecting the chancel was locked! So this 'document entrusted to Providence' and to 'the God of truth and justice, the protector of the oppressed', as Rousseau put it in the page added to the manuscript at the last moment, appeared likely after all to fall into the hands of his enemies. After leaving the cathedral he wandered about the streets of Paris, finally returning home in a state of exhaustion. Still tormented by anxiety, he hastily penned a leaflet addressed 'To any Frenchman still loving justice and truth', in which he asked once more to be informed of his crimes and to know 'how and by whom he had been judged'. His desperation was intensified by the thought that he was 'an unfortunate foreigner, alone, at their mercy, without support or defence', a man who could only 'raise to Heaven for his complete defence a heart without deceit and hands pure of all evil' (I, 990). When he tried to distribute his leaflet to passers-by, they refused to take it or merely observed, after glancing at the title, that it 'was not addressed to them'. He was equally dissatisfied with the response of those to whom he sent it. Then, quite suddenly, he decided 'to withdraw into himself' and examine the reality of his own being, only to find that the terrible persecution to which he was being subjected had not altered his essential character; although 'they make a Jean-Jacques in their fashion, Rousseau will always remain the same in spite of them'. For most of his life he had been conscious of the power of another person's look and now, for the first time, he felt himself to be free from its influence. 'Is the essence of my being', he asks in a striking expression, 'in their looks?' (I, 985). How can another's look affect 'the testimony of his own conscience?' 'Detached from all earthly things' and from 'the mad judgement of men', he henceforth has to seek a different kind of 'felicity'. 'Detached from all earthly affection and even delivered from the anxiety of hope, I no longer see any means by which they can disturb the peace of my heart'. He insists that this mood of resignation, already evident at the end of the *Dialogues*, will now be transformed into 'a permanent state from which nothing will any longer be able to draw him'. Heaven would do its work: of that he was sure, but he had been wrong to try to fix the time and the means. 'What I know is that the supreme judge is powerful and just, that my soul is innocent and that I have not deserved my fate' (I, 989).

Soon after his return to Paris, Rousseau had found a partial escape from his anxieties and tensions by again taking up a former hobby — botany. He dropped it in 1773, perhaps because his energies were being devoted to the composition of the *Dialogues*, but in 1777 he returned to it once more and it remained one of his chief interests until the end of his life. After he had left Paris in May 1778 to go and live on the estate of the Marquis de Girardin at Ermenonville, he was able to botanise in the large park and he seems to have become so completely engrossed in his hobby that he finally gave up nearly every other activity. One of the reasons for his love of botany was the opportunity it gave him for walking in the countryside. Although he was occasionally accompanied by a friend such as Bernardin de Saint-Pierre, he usually preferred to be alone. He still needed to reflect upon the meaning of his life and character and, more important still, to feel the reality of his own existence. 'These hours of solitude and meditation are the only ones in the day when I am fully myself, and belong to myself without diversion and obstacle, and when I can truly say that I am what nature wanted' (I, 1002).

It was during these walks in the countryside around Paris that he conceived the idea of his last — and in many ways most beautiful, though unfinished — work, *Les Rêveries du Promeneur Solitaire* (*The Reveries of the Lonely Walker*).[4] While walking he would jot down some of his thoughts on the back of playing-cards, developing them in a more formal way when he returned home. The work consists of a series of *Promenades* or *Walks*, which are essays on themes drawn from his personal life. The emotional tone is, for the most part, more restrained and diffused than in the other personal writings because the author is no longer concerned with recounting the story of his life and the 'secret history of his soul'; he is writing what he calls a 'shapeless diary'. By this he means that the work will not follow an overall systematic plan, for the subject-matter of each *Promenade* will be based on reflections which occur to him on his daily walks. Nevertheless, he claims that his writing will not lack precision, since he is proposing 'to take account of the modifications of his soul and their successions' (I, 1000). 'I shall carry out on myself the operations made by physicists on the air in order to know its daily state. I shall apply the barometer to my soul' and 'I shall be content to keep the register of the operations without reducing them to a system'. The pursuit of self-knowledge, so important in the *Confessions*, will thus be maintained in the *Reveries*: the author is seeking 'new knowledge of his nature and his moods' through an analysis of the 'feelings and thoughts of which his soul makes its daily sustenance in his present strange position'. All this is perhaps not surprising in someone who has tried 'to know his nature and the purpose of his existence with more tenacity and earnestness than any other man'. He 'has sought to direct the use of his life to knowing its end' and, with that intention, he claims to have undertaken 'the most ardent and sincere researches which perhaps have ever been made by any mortal' (I, 1017).

It is astonishing that a writer who has already spent so much time and effort upon the task of knowing and describing his true being in works as extensive as the *Confessions* and the *Dialogues* should still reveal the same preoccupation in the opening paragraph of his last work. 'What am I myself? This is what remains to be discovered.' Now, however, he is urged on less by a desperate desire to ward off the hostility of his ruthless enemies than by the thought that he is approaching the end of his life. This explains why he is writing for himself rather than for others. He feels that the time is fast approaching when he will have to present God with an account of his life's steward-ship: 'I devote my last days to studying myself and preparing in advance the account that I shall soon have to give of myself' (I, 999). This last work is being written in the shadow of eternity; the 'fate of his soul' is at stake. Although religion may not be the main theme of the work, Rousseau is constantly aware of the watchful presence of Providence. If he now suffers, it is because God wishes him to do so for His own inscrutable reasons; Jean-Jacques must bow to the divine will, comforted by the expectation that the day will come 'sooner or later' when order will be restored.

Yet all his attempts to attain deeper knowledge of himself and to effect a moral improvement cannot be detached from the anguish of being the object of universal hatred; he cannot escape from his deeply rooted conviction that he is a good and innocent man persecuted by ruthless enemies. This polaris-ation of diametrically opposed attitudes is now a permanent feature of his inner life: he needs his persecutors to sustain the notion of his own innocence. He believes that his enemies will persist in seeing 'the J.J. they have made for themselves in accordance with their own hearts' (I, 1059), and that they will not hesitate to present him as a 'monster, murderer, poisoner, or else an object of loathing and contempt spat upon by passers-by'. Usually they do not dare to come out into the open but 'burrow under the ground like moles'. It is very difficult for him to ignore the inescapable presence of evil men bent on his defamation and destruction. 'The traitors are silently entang-ling him in nets forged in the depths of hell' and the 'refine-ments of their hatred' are as 'immortal as the demon inspiring it'. When his enemies are not hiding in subterranean darkness, they are like wild beasts. He now believes that the only wise attitude is to treat them as 'strangers, unknown people, nobodies'; he seeks to take away their human characteristics by transforming them into 'mechanical beings acting only by physical impulsion'; they are mere 'differently moved masses devoid, as far as he is concerned, of all human morality' (I,

1078). In such a situation there is little he can do except submit to a 'pure fatality which has neither direction, intention nor moral cause': he is a purely passive being who can no longer resist his 'destiny'. For the most part he has (in an expression already used at the end of the *Dialogues*) 'delivered himself from the anxiety of hope' and with resignation he has found 'peace of soul'. 'All other old men worry about everything: I worry about nothing.' Ironically, he finds that it is his ruthless enemies who, by overreaching themselves and depriving him of all hope, have brought him that very peace which they are constantly seeking to deny him.

The habit of looking at his own uniquely desperate situation with an air of melancholy resignation gives a tone of pathos to much of Rousseau's writing and even imbues it with an element of poetic lyricism. 'Here I am, then, alone on earth, no longer having any other brother, neighbour, friend or company but myself. The most sociable and loving of men has been banished by an unanimous agreement.' Or again: 'Everything is over for me on earth. People can no longer do me either good or evil. There remains nothing more for me to hope for or fear in this world, and here I am, calm in the bottom of the abyss, a poor unhappy mortal but as impassive as God himself' (I, 999).

Being no longer obsessed by the thought of his persecutors — or, rather, the idea of persecution having now been accepted by him as part of his normal life — he can henceforth direct his thoughts and feelings upon himself, not simply with a view to furthering self-knowledge, but also in order to find a new basis for personal fulfilment. The very fact of his absolute isolation leads him to recognize that he must henceforth 'rely on himself for his only resources'. Since 'our happiness is within us', he must 'feed on his own substance' and he is all the more willing to do so when he realizes that this is 'inexhaustible'. This explains why he is no longer tormented by the anxiety previously aroused by the *Confessions* and *Dialogues*. 'Let people spy on what I am doing, let them worry about these sheets, let them seize them, suppress them or falsify them, I am henceforth indifferent to it all' (I, 1001). Unlike the *Confessions* which, as their very title suggests, were addressed to other people, the *Reveries* are a form of inner communion, the record of a lonely man 'conversing with his soul' and recounting these intimate conversations for his own pleasure.

As the objective embodiment of personal thoughts and feelings, the written word will be, he hopes, a particularly effective source of contentment, for 'the reading of them [his *Reveries*] will recall the pleasure I enjoy in writing them and thus resurrecting past time, they will so to speak double my existence. In spite of men I shall still know how to enjoy the charm of company and, though decrepit, I shall live with myself in another age, as I should live with a friend less old' (I, 1001). In this way he hopes to provide his existence with a more solid foundation than the fleeting experiences of daily life; he is seeking a happiness that is a 'permanent and simple state' and not a series of intense but transitory moments of pleasure and he is convinced that the calm perusal of his own recorded reflections can bring him this enduring satisfaction. However, in spite of this effort to give his life a stable basis, Rousseau believes that complete happiness can be achieved only by raising himself above the normal limitations and vagaries of everyday experience: he dreams of a self-realisation characterised by an absolute plenitude of consciousness: if he loves solitude, it is because it lets him enjoy the reality of his own being 'fully, without diversion and without obstacle' (I, 1002), so that he can say that he has 'truly lived' and been 'what nature wanted' (I, 1099). The Savoyard priest had expressed the same sentiment when he meditated on his existence in the next world: 'I aspire to the moment when, freed from the shackles of the body, I shall be myself without contradiction and without sharing and shall need only myself to be happy' (IV, 604-5).

Yet such moments are rare and usually unpredictable. Such certainly was the case when Rousseau attained a new level of experience after being knocked unconscious by a large dog during a walk on 24 October 1776. When he regained his senses, he had lost all memory of his individual existence and all feeling of pain. It was as though he 'were being born to life at that moment'. He enjoyed an extraordinary sense of personal expansion and seemed to 'fill all the objects he perceived with his light existence'. 'Completely given to the present moment, I remembered nothing; I had no distinct notion of my individuality, not the least idea of what had just happened to me; I did not know who I was or where I was; I felt neither pain, fear nor anxiety. I watched my blood flowing as I should have watched a stream, without thinking that this blood was in any way mine. I felt in my whole being a ravishing calm to which, whenever I remember it, I find nothing comparable in all the activity of known pleasures' (I, 1005). The attraction of this experience was undoubtedly the feeling of absolute inner plenitude, of being freed from any kind of inner division or conflict.

After arousing the hostility of the local clergy, and especially after having had stones thrown at his house, Rousseau fled from Môtiers in 1765 and sought refuge on the Isle de Saint-Pierre where he had a short but idyllic sojourn in the late summer of that year. This delightfully 'circumscribed' island, with a 'romantic' setting so admirably suited to 'the happiness of a man who loved to circumscribe himself', enabled him to obtain a brief glimpse of perfect happiness. Normally obsessed by the thought that 'everything is in a continuous flux on earth', he would be, like most men, 'always ahead or behind himself, recalling a past which existed no longer or anticipating a future which often was not to be, so that there was nothing to which the heart could be attached'; at most he could experience 'a fleeting state which still leaves the heart anxious and empty, which makes us regret something before, or yet desire something after'. At last he had been able to overcome this limitation by finding 'a state solid enough for his soul to be able to rest completely in it and gather there its whole being, without needing to recall the past or encroach on the future; in which time does not exist for it [the soul], in which the present still endures without none the less marking its duration and without any trace of succession, without any other feeling of privation or enjoyment, desire or fear than that of our existence, and this feeling alone can fill it completely' (I, 1046).

In this higher plane of consciousness Rousseau is not striving for some ineffable religious experience, for he is not trying to overcome time as such, but only the temporal divisions of everyday life: he is seeking a present which embraces both past and future, so that the present itself is expanded into an 'eternal moment'. Reverie thus becomes the supreme expression of that immediate experience by which Rousseau had always set so much store: he had never longed for the enjoyment of 'distant vistas' but had always sought a satisfaction which was within his immediate reach. On the Isle de Saint-Pierre this aspiration found complete fulfilment in the pure 'feeling of existence': an absolute and ultimately indescribable form of consciousness that went beyond the possibility of analysis or reflection and offered the experience of perfect self-realization. So perfect was the experience that it seemed to be endowed with a divine self-sufficiency. In the state of reverie, concludes Rousseau, 'one is self-sufficient like God'.

This experience was independent of any particular environment and could be obtained in any quiet place. 'I have often thought that in the Bastille or in a dungeon where my gaze encountered no object I could still have engaged in pleasant reverie' (I, 1048). Nevertheless, the pleasure of reverie could be immeasurably increased when it took place in a congenial setting, especially in a 'circumscribed island separated from the rest of the world'. The presence of physical nature could provide conditions which protected the inner self from all unwelcome distractions: more especially, the sensuous and affective aspects of the personality could be 'lulled' by the gentle rhythmic 'rocking' of water, and a mental state in which thoughts flitted across the surface of the mind was often enough to prevent it from sinking into mere torpor; in this way personal consciousness could be released for the enjoyment of its own existence.

Perhaps the perfection of reverie as described in the fifth *Promenade* owes something to the act of recapturing it through writing and so of using idealised memories. In any case, Rousseau recognizes that he is now too old to enjoy the pure reverie of the Isle de Saint-Pierre and that he must be content with a less exalted form: he will henceforth make use of his imagination. At times he indulges in sheer fantasy — for example, in the sixth *Promenade* when for a time he imagines himself capable of the invisibility provided by Gyges' ring; on another occasion he lets himself be carried up on the 'wings of his imagination' to the ethereal regions where he will one day be allowed to converse with the 'celestial intelligences' (I, 1049). To the activity of his imagination will be added memories of past happiness, for which he has a particularly strong predilection.

However alluring the power of imagination and memory may be, Rousseau recognizes that it cannot be a complete substitute for contact with reality and especially the physical nature he has loved since childhood. True happiness would be impossible without the beauty of the countryside. Far from being exclusively concerned with lonely self-communings, the *Reveries* reveal Rousseau again responding to the beauty of the physical world. He recalls his earlier days when he 'threw himself headlong into the ocean of nature' and his soul could 'wander and hover in the universe on the wings of imagination in ecstasies which surpassed any other enjoyment' (I, 1066). He would 'lose himself with a delightful intoxication in the immensity of this beautiful system with which he felt himself to be identified'. At such times all 'particular objects escaped him: he saw and felt nothing save in the whole'. 'I feel inexpressible raptures and ecstasies as I merge to to speak in the system of beings and identify myelf with the whole of nature.' With his physical decline, however, he is no longer able to experience such intense emotions and he has to be satisfied with less exalted enjoyment. Yet he still feels close to nature and 'taking refuge with the common mother, I have tried to escape in her arms from the assaults of her children' (I, 1063-6). 'I see only animosity on men's faces, and nature always smiles at me' (I, 1095). Sometimes he is content to feel an emotional affinity with the physical world: a melancholy autumn landscape inevitably reminds him that he too is in the autumn of his life and that the death-like coldness of winter is not so far away.

In spite of the emotional satisfaction derived from his relationship with the physical world, Rousseau is now aware of being 'dominated by his senses' and the vivacity of his 'sensations'. He can rejoice in the freshness of a scene which exudes an almost nuptial charm as he contemplates nature adorned in her bridal gown. The beauty of flowers and plants is always there to purify his imagination. Although his soul is henceforth dead to the 'great movements' which used to raise it to ecstatic heights, his senses continue to respond to the attraction of 'brilliant flowers, the variegated hues of the meadows, fresh shades, streams, groves and verdure'. Whereas he was formerly drawn to the majesty of the whole and was accustomed to look at nature 'as a mass', he now takes pleasure in examining it more closely and in greater detail. This is the main attraction he finds in botanising: he can wander from one object to another, examining them 'with interest and curiosity' and feeling that he is beyond the reach of wicked people: he is 'forgotten, free and peaceful as though he had no more enemies and the foliage of the woods protected him from their attacks'. If botany appeals to a man 'dominated by the powerful impression of objects', it also offers him a pastime which satisfies his desire for simple innocent pleasures. Moreover, as his physical strength declines, he can always relive some of his most delightful memories by contemplating the herbarium he has formed, for this constitutes the 'diary' of his expeditions. As he looks at his collection of plants and flowers, he remembers 'both his youth and his innocent pleasures' and so enjoys them once again 'in the midst of the saddest fate to which any mortal has ever had to submit' (I, 1073). Indeed, so great was the attraction of his hobby that it eventually replaced the writing of his reveries.

His reactions to physical nature still retain a strong religious element and his response to the beauty of the 'universal system' continues to be bound up with his firmly held conviction that it is God's handiwork. The long history of his religious development recorded in the third *Promenade* culminates in a synthesis which affirms a close correspondence between the spiritual significance of the physical universe and that of man himself: Rousseau perceives a 'congruity' between his 'immortal nature and the constitution of this world and the corresponding moral order' (I, 1018-9). He thereby re-affirms a principle developed more fully in his formal religious writings. In any case, he has no doubt that all the vital aspects of man's being take him towards God. 'Meditation in seclusion, the study of nature, the contemplation of the universe, impel a lonely man to move constantly towards the author of things and to seek with a gentle concern the end of all he sees and the cause of all he feels' (I, 1014).

At certain times Rousseau believes that his own life has given him insight into the essence of God's being: his enemies have driven him into a situation where he feels as 'impassive as

God himself'. Even more remarkable is the experience of God-like self-sufficiency in the state of reverie, to which reference has already been made. Religious themes and feelings thus emerge at different points in the *Reveries* in accordance with the author's changing moods and, in spite of their link with his reaction to the physical world, are closely related to the demands of his inner life: conscious of the mysterious workings of Providence, he dwells more and more on the idea of immortality and on the thought that the divine order which men have disturbed in this world will be restored in the next.

However deep the satisfaction provided by lonely reverie, his response to the beauty of the divine creation and his own religious feelings, Rousseau cannot forget his need for human beings. Already in the *Dialogues* he had made the surprising admission that his love of nature was only a 'substitute' for human affection. In that work he had spoken of his 'devouring' need to love and be loved. At the very beginning of the *Reveries* he describes himself as the 'most sociable and loving of men' and he goes on to maintain that it is men who have rejected him, not he who has rejected them. His unwitting dependence on others is revealed by his frequent references to his deter-mination to be happy 'in spite of them'. 'I should have loved men', he declares, 'in spite of themselves', but they will no longer prevent him from 'enjoying his innocence and ending his days in peace in spite of them' (I, 996-1001). The ambiv-alence of his attitude is revealed when, during one of his botanising excursions in the Swiss mountains, he suddenly comes across a stocking-manufacturer. 'I cannot express the confused and contradictory agitation I felt in my heart at this discovery.' 'My first impulse was a feeling of joy at finding myself once more among human beings when I had believed myself to be absolutely alone' (I, 1071). Soon this feeling of joy gave way to a more painful reaction as he realised that even in 'the very caverns of the Alps' he could not escape from 'the cruel hands of men eager to torment him'. Although initial pleasure experienced at the sight of others was usually fol-lowed by a mood of mistrust, he could not completely over-come his need for them. He was particularly happy when he found himself in the company of simple people — whether old or young — and when he could see happiness in their faces. He

171

recounts his delight at providing some inexpensive pleasure for a company of schoolgirls and the contentment he derived from talking to the military pensioners of Les Invalides.

This need for human affection and companionship at a deeper and more intimate level is strikingly revealed in his very last pages, which are devoted to an unfinished *Promenade* recalling his earlier life with Mme de Warens, the only woman who left a permanent impression on his emotional life. 'Ah!', he cries pathetically, 'if only I had been sufficient for her heart as she was for mine! What peaceful and delightful days we should have spent together!' This was a period when he was 'fully himself, without admixture and without obstacle' — a 'short but precious moment in his life' when he could give way to 'expansive and tender feelings'. 'A lonely house on a valley-slope was our refuge and it is there in the space of four or five years that I enjoyed a century of life and a pure full happiness which covers with charm all the frightfulness of my present fate' (I, 1099).

To the question 'What am I?' Rousseau persists in giving the direct answer: 'A good and innocent man persecuted by a wicked world'. Yet the irrepressible activity of reflection and the need to be constantly taking up his pen — as well as the revelations of the text itself — prove that he was not entirely satisfied with this straightforward response or the simple image which he had previously hoped other people would accept as that of his true self. In spite of his repeated claim that there was nothing reprehensible in his heart, a long piece of sophistical reasoning such as the fourth *Promenade*, which purports to deal objectively with the problem of lying, shows that his mind is not at peace, for the abstract arguments cannot prevent him from referring indirectly to the feelings of guilt associated with the abandonment of his children. In another *Promenade* he acknowledges that he is not as virtuous as he once believed and that it is not enough to be merely 'good' when goodness requires no more than the spontaneous effusion of innate feelings, whereas virtue requires a determined act of will.

Such doubts and hesitations — as well as the ambivalence of his attitude towards people — are not enough to affect his deeply held conviction that it is not possible for others to change his essential being and that, in spite of his enemies' 'power and veiled intrigues', 'he would continue, whatever they did, to be what he was in spite of them'. His ultimate aim was to be a stable fulfilled being, 'happy and content, without diversion, without obstacle' (I, 1082) and enjoying 'a pure, full happiness'. It is because they express such intimate longings and emotions that the *Reveries* are imbued with a quasi-poetic charm; a gentle musical response is often discernible in a prose that follows the innermost movements of the writer's heart.

Whether Rousseau finally achieved his aim of finding inner peace we cannot tell. During the last months of his life — in fact, on May 20 1778 — he left Paris for the estate of the Marquis de Girardin at Ermenonville. It was to be his last move. More important still, it had been preceded by a decision to give up writing. On April 12 he had begun his last *Promenade* which he was to leave unfinished. At Ermenonville he was content to go for walks in the park and indulge in his favourite pastime of botanising. It was on his return from one of these walks on July 2 1778 that he suddenly collapsed and died.

Conclusion

Rousseau was of his age and yet against it; in some respects too he was ahead of it, so that he is both the representative of a dying order and the precursor of a new one. As a self-educated Genevan Protestant endowed with a highly sensitive temperament, he never accepted the French environment in which he spent so much of his adult life: though attracted by its refined taste and superficial brilliance, he was repelled by its moral decadence. From the outset of a literary career that began almost by accident in early middle-age, he emerged as an apparently uncompromising critic of contemporary society; to this view the personal writings added the image of a good and lonely man persecuted by a hostile and uncomprehending world, and it was this Rousseau which many later readers, more familiar with the *Confessions* than with *Emile*, accepted as the true one. The Romantics, in particular, held out a fraternal hand to a writer who had so effectively expressed their own sense of estrangement from society. Rousseau, it seemed, had called men back to the reality of their own being at a time when it was being stifled or corrupted by their artificial environment.

Always likely to arouse strong feelings in others, he himself rarely discouraged such a reaction, for he feared nothing so much as indifference. 'Whoever is not passionately for me,' he declared in words reminiscent of Jesus, 'is not worthy of me'. In the *Confessions* he readily admitted that he would 'rather be forgotten by the whole human race than be considered an ordinary man' (I, 1123). In this respect, at least, posterity has not disappointed his expectation, for it has either extolled the man for his virtue or blamed him for his vices, lauded his work for its moral elevation or denounced its insidious capacity for corruption. Rousseau himself also insisted that there was an indissoluble link between a writer's character and his work: in his opinion, a good man dedicated (like himself) to the cause of

God and humanity could not produce a morally bad book. This probably explains his acute anxiety over the fate of works such as *Emile* and the *Confessions* into which he had put the best of himself as man and author; it was by these expressions of his essential being that he wished ultimately to be judged. Likewise, he saw in the beneficent emotional effects of *La Nouvelle Héloïse* an incontrovertible proof of his own loving nature; it would be impossible, he averred, for a misanthropic man to have spoken of love in such glowing terms. Whether he was writing for his contemporaries or himself, Rousseau was always imbued with a great earnestness, believing that literature ought to have a worthwhile moral purpose and deal with ideas which were for the good of humanity.

If Rousseau stressed the personal basis of ideas which evoked the vision of 'a new man and a new universe', this did not prevent him from being involved in the intellectual controversies of his day; in spite of his deeply held convictions, he carefully pondered the ideas of other writers. While still a youth, he had been so deeply conscious of his own lack of formal education that he made a determined and prolonged effort to build 'a storehouse of ideas' and, as the *Confessions* make clear, this process of self-education led him to study many authors, both ancient and modern. Scholars have carefully examined his relationship to the works he read at this time, and one aim of the present study has been to relate many of Rousseau's ideas to traditions with which he was familiar. At the same time it is important to recognize that undue attention to detailed sources is apt to be misleading if no account is taken of Rousseau's main intentions. It was thus typical not only of his contemporaries but also of many later critics that they treated the first *Discourse* as little more than a brilliant paradox; they were made uneasy or hostile as soon as they realized that Rousseau believed passionately in the truth of his ideas.

In view of the many echoes of other writers in his work, it is pertinent to ask where his originality really lies. The preceding analysis will already have shown that Rousseau saw himself first of all at an uncompromising opponent of contemporary society and culture. The *philosophes*, it is true, were also very critical of several aspects of the existing order and Voltaire, in particular, was ready to take active steps to oppose and redress gross miscarriages of justice. Yet, in their case, it was a question of calling attention to particular abuses and of making society more rational, tolerant and human. Rousseau, on the other hand, rarely intervened in specific issues (he was reluctant, for example, to be involved in efforts to improve the lot of persecuted French Protestants), preferring to concentrate on what he described as 'general and useful truths', but these led him to undertake a radical re-appraisal of the social and cultural values of his day.

In a sense Rousseau's initial attitude was not dissimilar from that of Descartes, inasmuch as he too affirmed that thinkers should free themselves from old prejudices and traditions and start again. Unlike Descartes, however, who had carried out a purely intellectual revolution based on the indisputable authority of reason, Rousseau's criticism of culture and society eventually involved him in a fundamental re-examination of man's being: he came to see that it was not enough to make a purely rational analysis of human nature; it was equally important to take into account its affective elements. In other words, while not denying the importance of reason, he insisted that it had to be related to other and perhaps more fundamental aspects of human experience. Although the *philosophes* had already rejected traditional metaphysics in favour of some form of Locke-inspired empiricism, the priority they accorded to sense-experience had led them either into psychological analysis (as in the case of Condillac) or — especially when to Locke's influence was added that of Newtonianism — into the scientific investigation of the physical world. If Rousseau sometimes referred to the scientific and psychological achievements of his age, his initial inspiration owed very little to them since he believed that his direct intuitive apprehension of reality gave him a much deeper understanding of human experience.

During recent decades some critics have treated Rousseau as one of the 'philosophers of existence', mainly because his fierce opposition to the cultural and social values of his time made him emphasize the supremacy of personal experience. In the *Profession of Faith*, the Savoyard priest locates the final goal of all human endeavour in 'the sheer delight which springs from contentment with oneself'. 'Supreme enjoyment', he declares, 'is in contentment with oneself.' Such an experience ultimately lies beyond the reach of language, for, as Rousseau affirms in the *Confessions*, true happiness is indescribable and he himself, as we have seen, considered the supreme moment of his own life to have been the occasion when he was able to enjoy an unalloyed and exalted 'feeling of existence'.

One cause of the immediate appeal of Rousseau's work, therefore, was probably the way it encouraged an age dominated by intellectual activity to rediscover the sources of an experience uncorrupted by artificial social and cultural influences. At a time when philosophical reflection often led to scepticism, Rousseau seemed to offer men a sound reason for accepting the reality of their own being. He was constantly encouraging them to withdraw into themselves (an expression that occurs in his first work as well as in his last) and discover their fundamental being. Although other thinkers like Locke, Condillac and Buffon were already adopting the genetic method, Rousseau, in spite of being indebted to them on detailed points, was not concerned primarily with the question of scientific or historical origins. At the beginning of the second *Discourse* he had announced his intention of 'putting aside facts', for he believed he could produce an imaginative hypothesis that would throw light on man's 'original' nature.

In Rousseau's opinion, his essentially child-like and innocent character made it possible for him to rely on his own intuition which, he was convinced, gave him direct access to truths concealed from his contemporaries. There is thus a 'primitivist' aspect to Rousseau's thought which sets it apart from the philosophies of his day and probably explains the fascination it has exerted over many generations of readers. Not only is he able to identify himself with the existence of primitive man in the second *Discourse*, or with that of the child in *Emile*, but he is constantly appealing for a return to the freshness, purity and innocence of 'original' experience. To those who are tired of intellectual sophistication he offers the glimpse of an 'earthly paradise' and a new 'golden age'. One particular theme that recurs constantly through his work is that of rebirth; he seems to offer men the possibility of starting life anew. In this respect it is not accidental that spring was his favourite season and dawn his favourite time of the day.

The theme of rebirth and the rediscovery of 'originality' are inseparable from his frequent reference to a principle popular with nearly all the philosophers of the Enlightenment: nature, a confused and confusing concept about which few could agree, although all acknowledged its supreme importance. Like many other thinkers of the time, Rousseau often uses 'nature' as a critical concept in order to suggest a reality that differs from the falsity of immediate 'appearance'. He did not disagree with those *philosophes* who preferred 'nature' to 'revelation' as the source of truth and insisted at the same time that nature and truth should be related to the search for happiness in the finite world. While being steadfastly opposed to philosophical materialism and scepticism, Rousseau believed that the principles of 'natural religion' could be found without the help of revelation since a man had only to make 'good use of his faculties' and rely on his 'eyes, conscience and judgment'. In Rousseau's opinion, this method had the unrivalled advantage of providing any sincere enquirer with a direct insight into the meaning of 'nature'. This is very apparent, for example, in ethical matters, since morality ultimately depends on the innate impulse or 'divine instinct' of conscience. Nature is thus transformed by Rousseau from an abstract philosophical concept into a living presence to which men can spontaneously respond because it is essentially 'good'; henceforth they will be able to see themselves as 'beings recently come forth from nature's hands'.

The opposition of a primordial, ideal nature to the corruption of modern life gives Rousseau's thought a strongly antithetical character, as is already clear from the resounding first sentences of *Emile* and the *Social Contract*. 'Everything is good as it comes forth from the Author of things, everything degenerates in man's hands.' 'Man was born free but is everywhere in chains.' Yet this appeal to the authentic source of human existence is not intended to be a mere escape into Utopia since it expresses God's original intention for mankind. As soon as they cease to be blinded by the limitations and defects of their present way of life, Rousseau insists that men will be able to transform a mere possibility into a genuinely personal reality.

Rousseau's eulogy of 'nature' has often caused him to be seen as an uncritical advocate of 'primitive life'. He himself, however, stressed the impossibility of returning to the past. 'Human nature never goes backwards and people can never return to the times of innocence and equality when they have left them' (I, 935). Men must be constantly moving forward to a new and higher stage of existence and the return to 'origins' is but a prelude to the search for a more mature form of existence. This is impossible without the use of all human powers, reason as well as feeling. In this respect, it may seem somewhat paradoxical to speak (as one critic has done) of Rousseau's 'rationalism' [1], but such a term can certainly serve as a useful corrective to an excessively emotional interpretation of his philosophy. In spite of his animadversions against the 'subtleties' of abstract metaphysics, Rousseau's emphasis upon the notion of order made him sympathetic to the broad metaphysical tradition which strove to discover a rational meaning in the structure of reality as a whole. He was a great admirer of Plato and like him tried to find meaning in the system of the universe. As well as looking back to predecessors such as Plato and Malebranche, Rousseau was also indebted to less well-known writers, like the abbé de la Pluche and Father Bernard Lamy, who established a close link between the scientific and religious interpretation of the physical world. He was also familiar with early eighteenth-century deism; not only with the Cartesian and Newtonian form which involved the physico-mathematical conception of the physical world as a complex mechanism requiring God as its creator, but also with the deism deriving from a philosopher like Shaftesbury, who gave much greater prominence to feeling as a basic constituent in man's response to a divinely created order. Rousseau accords particular importance to the deism of Samuel Clarke whom on one occasion he compared to Plato.[2] Yet the language Rousseau uses to describe Clarke's thought is very revealing. After praising this system as 'the simplest and most reasonable philosophy' eminently suited for 'throwing light' on the meaning of the world, he goes on to extol it as 'great, consoling, sublime, capable of uplifting the soul and providing a foundation for virtue'; in other words, Clarke's deism satisfied both the affective and the rational side of human nature.

The way in which the link between reson and *sensibilité* awakened a new response to the physical world is very evident towards the end of the first part of the *Profession of Faith*, where the demands of man's inner life are related to his reactions to physical nature. Having established the rational basis of his religious philosophy, the individual is encouraged to raise himself to a higher plane of being by means of 'sublime contemplations'; he should 'meditate on the order of the universe not in order to explain it by futile systems but to admire it constantly, to adore the wise Author who is present in it'. Anyone who can achieve such deep and yet direct response to the divinely created universe will experience supreme bliss, 'for what sweeter bliss is there than to feel oneself part of a system in which everything is good?' Rousseau's personal writings also describe his ecstatic enjoyment as he identified himself with the majesty and beauty of the 'universal system'. At its most intense moments his feeling for nature obviously contained a powerful religious element.

Though not unaware that Rousseau's critical works raised fundamental questions about cultural values and the nature of man, many readers were so captivated by the vision of the 'new man' and the 'new world' he offered them, as well as by the magic of his style (to which even his enemies paid homage), that they responded more readily to his *sensibilité* than to his philosophical principles, for this was an aspect of his work that encouraged them to go beyond the essentially rational and intellectual outlook of the Enlightenment in order to renew their feeling for nature, revitalise their religious outlook and attain a fresh experience of life itself. Moreover, the glowing portrayal of love in the first part of *La Nouvelle Héloïse* reawakened many people — and especially women — to the needs of their heart and inner life. Although he may have been describing feelings that were beginning to appear in many aspects of European culture, Rousseau's particularly eloquent and powerful expression of this new *sensibilité* makes him an obvious precursor of Romanticism.

Yet an excessively 'Romantic' interpretation of his work, which stresses the affective to the exclusion of the rational aspects, gives a distorted view of his philosophy as a whole. The religious and metaphysical framework of his thought was strong enough to sustain his confidence not only in man's natural goodness but also in that of the universal system of which he formed part. Although at certain moments (as in the third letter to Malesherbes or in the later parts of his novel) Rousseau could express a longing for the infinite and stress the nothingness of human dreams, he never fell into the despair and pessimism of those Romantics who could not reconcile the infinite aspirations of their inner life with the inescapable mediocrity of finite existence. Even Rousseau's obsession with the idea that he was a good and innocent man persecuted by a wicked society never led him to doubt that (in his own words) 'sooner or later' God would bring back the order which lay at the heart of his creation; Jean-Jacques's unhappy isolation was but a strange aberration which in no way impugned the goodness of the universal system.

In spite of the prominence given to the principle of nature and man's innate goodness, and to his personal predilection for the spontaneous expression of feeling, Rousseau's conception of human existence as developing through various stages made him recognize that the uninhibited expression of emotion was not enough to form a complete philosophy of man; goodness had ultimately to give way to the needs of virtue. Even the infallible promptings of conscience as a special kind of feeling had to be clarified by reason and supported by the will. Any adequate moral philosophy, therefore, should recognize the importance of freedom as one of its cardinal principles; the power of the enlightened will, though sustained by conscience, presupposes man's ability to make effective choices and a major part of Rousseau's constructive thought, as we have seen, involves an analysis of freedom in the life of the individual and in political society.

Although there may be a tension between the rational and the affective — or, as Albert Schinz called it, the 'Roman' and the 'Romantic' — elements in Rousseau's thought, in so far as his own preference was for the spontaneous affirmation of man's natural goodness, he admitted that the existence of political obligations made it necessary for the individual to practise virtue and adopt moral principles which were as acceptable to his reason and will as to his heart. Yet, whatever its particular emphasis, Rousseau's thought as a whole tends to be dominated by the need for unity, for it is a philosophy of reconciliation: man is brought into harmony with his own essential being through the achievement of a unity and plenitude that eliminate the disquieting conflicts and contradictions of modern life. Moreover, this new-found harmony enables him to establish a meaningful relationship with the 'universal system' of which he forms part; he finds a close bond between his own unified self and the divinely created order to which it belongs. At the same time he cannot ignore his dependence on the social and political community through which he must also find moral fulfilment; in this case, however, he will rely on reason and will rather than on mere feeling, for political society, having been created by a deliberate decision, can survive only through the consent and support of its members.

Because human existence attains complete realization through the progressive and orderly development of all its powers, it is not surprising that freedom, though a dominant concept in Rousseau's work, is not a simple one. He carefully traces its growth from the 'natural' freedom of primitive man to the 'moral' freedom of the mature individual and the 'civil' freedom of the enlightened citizen. Although political freedom is given a strongly 'democratic' emphasis since it involves the absolute sovereignty of the people, Rousseau admits that the pressure of human selfishness and the tendency of organized societies to become a struggle between rich and poor, powerful and weak, may make it difficult for men to follow the prompting of their higher nature. He thus shows some ambiguity and hesitation in his proposals for putting his main principles into effect: we recall his recognition that men may be 'forced to be free', his tardy appeal to the idea of 'civil religion' and his use of an exceptional figure like the Lawgiver. However, Rousseau is not thinking of a dictator who imposes his arbitrary will on recalcitrant citizens, but of outstanding individuals who use their innate genius rather than any mere legal authority to help their fellow-men to achieve a full realization of their true nature.

The indissoluble link established by Rousseau between morality and politics means that it is impossible to include him in the liberal tradition. Although his view of freedom firmly opposes him to the absolutism of Hobbes, it does not align him with the liberalism of Locke, who assigned a protective rather than a morally formative influence to the State. By giving freedom a strictly moral basis Rousseau is also led to use the notion of equality as another indispensable political concept, for freedom must be for all; this, in turn, presupposes that the individual cannot be a virtuous citizen until he has achieved a disciplined and orderly relationship with other people. A democratic society, based on freedom and equality, cannot survive without the general acceptance of moral and political obligations, but Rousseau hopes that these will ultimately depend not on formal legislation but on the laws engraved in the citizens' own hearts. It is this concern with personal commitment which probably explains his own preference for the small, closely-knit and self-sufficient community whose members were all well known to one another.

Rousseau has sometimes been considered as the first 'modern man' and some support for this view is certainly to be found in both his life and his philosophy. The tragi-comedy of his quarrel with David Hume shows a lonely and sensitive man, immured in his fears and anxieties, confronting a typical representative of the Enlightenment, the benevolent religious sceptic who failed to understand the purpose of the wild accusations of deceit and treachery levelled against him by a man from whom he expected only friendship and gratitude. Moreover, Rousseau's tireless efforts to portray himself as a good and innocent man persecuted by a hostile world are to be found in personal writings which reveal the complexity and ambiguity not only of Jean-Jacques's own character but also of that of man himself. Rousseau's persistent advocacy of the principle of natural goodness in his didactic works did not prevent him — often unwittingly — from throwing into relief the darker and more irrational aspects of man's being. If in a still more general way his criticism of the artificial culture and society of his day led him to stress the idea of man's alienation from his true nature, this has persuaded some critics to include him among those thinkers who, like Nietzsche and Kierke-gaard, also denounced the soulless uniformity of a society that was robbing man of his real nature and personality.

In spite of the prophetic aspect of Rousseau's philosophy

there is one important sense in which it still belongs to the very Enlightenment of which, in other respects, it is so decisively critical. Like the *philosophes* — and unlike Kierkegaard or his French predecessor Pascal — Rousseau's thought lacks a tragic dimension. However unhappy he may have been in his own private life, his belief in natural goodness remained unshaken. Evil existed, no doubt, but it came to man from outside. Although the sight of humanity's present condition may convince us that 'men are wicked' — and Rousseau admitted that it may no longer be possible to reverse or even halt the grievous moral decline of large States — the fact that the evils of modern life have been due to historical causes, and not to original sin or innate perversity, means that it is still possible to inspire men with enough wisdom and courage for them to be able to accept the responsibility of shaping their own destiny. Rousseau believed that he had not only diagnosed the sickness of modern life, but that he had also offered his fellow-men an effective remedy by presenting them with a vision of their 'original' existence; as soon as they paid heed to his message, they could create a new unity and harmony in themselves and their environment.

Rousseau's view of freedom is very different from that of Kierkegaard and his existentialist followers. Although the Danish thinker stresses, like Rousseau, the three stages of existence — the 'aesthetic' (or 'natural'), moral and religious — he does so in a totally different manner. Whereas Rousseau believes that it is possible for the individual to move without difficulty from one stage to the next as long as he follows the direction of 'well-ordered nature', Kierkegaard treats the exercise of freedom as an occasion for 'dread': a higher stage cannot be reached except by a hazardous leap that opens up the possibility of nothingness as well as of fulfilment; freedom is inseparable from an anguished sense of personal responsibility which makes man feel that he is 'not at home' in the world or his own being. If, therefore, both thinkers consider that man's destiny is to exist 'before God', Rousseau believes that this can be achieved by following 'nature', whilst Kierkegaard insists on the supreme importance of a 'faith' that may involve the individual — as far as the human situation is concerned — in a sense of 'absurdity' and 'alienation'.

Conclusion

Although Rousseau was aware of the inner contradictions and tensions of modern man and constantly reproached him for being 'outside himself', he did not think that conflict and division were necessary to human existence; in his view it was possible to bring all the essential aspects of man's 'original' being into unity and harmony; as soon as he had established his proper relationship with nature, the individual could take his place in the universal system created by God. At the very centre of Rousseau's thought, therefore, is the firm conviction that happiness and self-realization are always attainable by those who have the wisdom to rise above the false values of corrupt society and to re-affirm their faith in the power of nature. To many, such an ideal has seemed dangerously utopian since it ignores the force of evil, but to others it has offered an inspiring goal for all worthwhile human endeavour. In any case such is the power of Rousseau's literary genius that his work still continues to occupy those who, though disagreeing on its ultimate value, consider it relevant to any serious effort to elaborate a genuine 'philosophy of man'.

Notes

CHAPTER 1. ROUSSEAU AND THE FRENCH ENLIGHTENMENT

1 All references indicated solely by volume and page-number are to the *Oeuvres complètes de Jean-Jacques Rousseau*, ed. B. Gagnebin and M. Raymond (Bibliothèque de la Plèïade), Paris, Vols. I-IV, Paris, 1959-70.

2 All references to Rousseau's correspondence (indicated as *CC*, with volume and page-number) are to the *Correspondance complète de Jean-Jacques Rousseau*, edited by R. A. Leigh, Geneva and Oxford, 1965 (in course of publication).

3 Voltaire, *Lettres philosophiques*, especially letters 14-16.

4 Cf. Voltaire, op. cit., Letter 13; Locke, *Essay concerning Human Understanding*, Book IV, Chapter xix, 7.

5 The three accounts are to be found in the second of the *Quatre Lettres à M. de Malesherbes* (I, 1135-6), Book VII of the *Confessions* (I, 350-2) and the second of the *Dialogues: Rousseau juge de Jean-Jacques* (I, 828-9).

CHAPTER 2. THE RETURN TO ORIGINS

1 A detailed analysis of Rousseau's relationship with the Natural Right tradition is to be found in R. Derathé's *Rousseau et la science politique de son temps*, Paris, 1950. See also my essay, 'Some Aspects of the Theory of Natural Right', in *From Montesquieu to Laclos: Studies of the French Enlightenment*, Geneva, 1974, Chapter VIII, pp. 93-108.

2 Further details are to be found in the editor's notes, III, 1295-6.

3 For the earlier history of controversy see Margaret Moffat, *Rousseau et la querelle du théâtre au XVIIIᵉ siècle*, 1930.

4 As the *Lettre à d'Alembert sur les Spectacles* has not yet been included in the *Oeuvres complètes*, all references are to the critical edition by M. Fuchs, Lille and Geneva, 1948.

CHAPTER 3. THE NEW MAN

1 See Jean Chateau: *Jean-Jacques Rousseau, sa philosophie de l'éducation*, Paris, 1962, and C. H. Dobinson: *Jean-Jacques Rousseau* (Library of Educational Thought), London, 1969.

2 See above p. 29.

3 Clarke had also made a considerable impression on Voltaire. Cf. the interesting article by W. H. Barber, 'Voltaire and Samuel Clarke', in *Studies on Voltaire and the Eighteenth Century*, Vol. 179, 1979, 47-61.

4 For the textual aspect see P. M. Masson's critical edition of *La Profession de foi du vicaire savoyard de Jean-Jacques Rousseau*, Fribourg and Paris, 1914, and for other aspects of the work the same author's *La Religion de Jean-Jacques Rousseau*, 3 vols., Paris, 1916, and my own *Rousseau and the Religious Quest*, Oxford, 1968.
5 Quoted in P. Burgelin, *La Philosophie de l'Existence de J.-J. Rousseau*, Paris, 1952, p. 319.

CHAPTER 4. EMOTION AND MORALITY

1 M.B.Ellis, *Julie or La Nouvelle Héloïse: A Synthesis of Rousseau's Thought, 1749-59*, Toronto, 1949.
2 See the introduction and notes to Daniel Mornet's edition of *La Nouvelle Héloïse*, Les Grands Ecrivains de la France, 4 vols., Paris, 1925.

CHAPTER 5. THE NEW CITIZEN

1 Cf. C.E. Vaughan's edition of *Du Contrat social ou Principes du droit politique*, Manchester, 1918. A detailed consideration of the work and notes on specific points in the text are to be found in my edition of *Du Contrat social* (with introduction and notes in English), Oxford, 1972.
2 See above p. 91.

CHAPTER 6. PRACTICAL POLITICS

1 See Michel Launay, *Jean-Jacques Rousseau: écrivain politique, 1712-62*, Cannes and Grenoble, 1971.
2 Op. cit., Chapter II.
3 See Jean-Daniel Candaux's introduction in III, clix-cxcviii, for the background and history of the controversy.
4 The text is given in III, 901-950. See also the introduction by Sven Stelling-Michaud, III, cxcix-ccxiii.
5 The text of the *Considérations* is given in III, 951-1041, with an informative introduction by Jean Fabre, III, ccxvi-ccxliii.
6 See above p. 92.
7 There is a similar description of the *Montagnons* in the *Lettre à d'Alembert sur les Spectacles*, pp. 80-83. See above p. 41.

CHAPTER 7. PHILOSOPHY AND THE INDIVIDUAL

1 The text of the letters is to be found in I, 1130-47.
2 See above p. 14.
3 Cf. Ronald Grimsley, *Jean-Jacques Rousseau: A Study in Self-Awareness*, Cardiff, 2nd ed. 1969; W.H. Blanchard, *Rousseau and the Spirit of Revolt: A Psychological Study*, Michigan, 1967.
4 There is an English translation, *Reveries of the Solitary Walker*, by Peter France, Penguin Books, Harmondsworth, 1979.

CONCLUSION

1 Cf. Robert Derathé, *Le Rationalisme de Rousseau*, Paris, 1948.
2 IV, 1135.

Bibliography

For Rousseau's biography the reader is referred to the following works:

Green, F.C., *Jean-Jacques Rousseau*, Cambridge, 1955.
Guéhenno, J., *Jean-Jacques Rousseau*: translated by J. and D. Weightman, 2 vols. London, 1966 (The original was entitled *Jean-Jacques*, 3 vols., Paris, 1940-52 and then, in 2 vols., *Jean-Jacques: histoire d'une conscience*, Paris, 1962).
Crocker, L.G., *J.-J. Rousseau*, 2 vols., New York, 1968-73.
Huizinga, J.H., *The Making of a Saint: the Tragi-comedy of J.-J. Rousseau*, London, 1975.

Of the numerous books devoted to Rousseau's work the following are particularly relevant to the present study:

Broome, J.H., *Rousseau: A Study of his Thought*, London, 1963
Burgelin, P., *La Philosophie de l'Existence de J.-J. Rousseau*, Paris, 1950
Cassirer, E., *The Question of Jean-Jacques Rousseau*, trans. P. Gay, New York, 1962.
De Beer, G., *J.-J. Rousseau and his World*, London, 1972.
Blanchard, W.H., *Rousseau and the Spirit of Revolt: A Psychological Study*, Michigan, 1967.
Charvet, J., *The Social Problem in the Philosophy of Rousseau*, Cambridge, 1974.
Cobban, A., *Rousseau and the Modern State*, new ed., London, 1964.
Crocker, L.G., *Rousseau's Social Contract: an interpretive essay*, Cleveland, 1968.
Derathé, R., *Le Rationalisme de Rousseau*, Paris, 1948. *Rousseau et la science politique de son temps*, Paris, 1950.
Ellenburg, S., *Rousseau's Political Philosophy: An Interpretation from Within*, Ithaca, New York, 1976.
Ellis, M.B., *Julie or La Nouvelle Héloïse, A Synthesis of Rousseau's Thought, 1749-59*, Toronto, 1949. *Rousseau's Socratic Aemilian*

myths: a literary collation of 'Emile' and the 'Social Contract', Columbus, Ohio, 1980.

Gagnebin, B., *A la rencontre de Jean-Jacques Rousseau*, Geneva, 1962.

Grimsley, R., *Jean-Jacques Rousseau: A Study in Self-Awareness*, new ed., Cardiff, 1969. *The Philosophy of Rousseau*, London, 1973. *Rousseau and the Religious Quest*, Oxford, 1968.

Hall, J.C., *Rousseau; an Introduction to his Political Philosophy*, London, 1973.

Hendel, C.W., *Jean-Jacques Rousseau Moralist*, 2 vols., London, 1934.

Launay, M., *J.-J. Rousseau: écrivain politique, 1712-62*, Geneva, 1971.

McDonald, J., *Rousseau and the French Revolution*, London, 1965.

Masson, P.M., *La Religion de Rousseau*, 3 vols., 2nd ed., Paris, 1916.

Masters, R.D., *The Political Philosophy of J.-J. Rousseau*, Princeton, 1968.

May, G., *Rousseau par lui-même*, Paris, 1961.

Mornet, D., *Rousseau, l'homme et l'oeuvre*, Paris, 1950.

Raymond, M., *Jean-Jacques Rousseau, la quête de soi et la rêverie*, Paris, 1962.

Roddier, H., *J.-J. Rousseau en Angleterre au XVIIIe siècle*, Paris, 1950.

Roussel, J., *J.-J. Rousseau en France après la Révolution, 1795-1830*, Paris, 1972.

Schinz, A., *La Pensée de Jean-Jacques Rousseau*, Paris, 1929.

Shklar, J., *Men and Citizens: A Study of Rousseau's Social Theory*, Cambridge, 1969.

Spink, J.S., *Rousseau et Genève*, Paris, 1935.

Starobinski, J., *Jean-Jacques Rousseau: la transparence et l'obstacle*, new ed., Paris, 1970.

Trousson, J., *Rousseau et sa fortune littéraire*, Paris, 1971.

Voisine, J., *J.-J. Rousseau en Angleterre à l'époque romantique*, Paris, 1956.

Wright, E.H., *The Meaning of Rousseau*, London, 1929.

Index